P9-CLS-994

3d Edition

The Complete Guide to
Trail Building
and Maintenance

Carl Demrow & David Salisbury

APPALACHIAN MOUNTAIN CLUB BOOKS
BOSTON, MASSACHUSETTS

Cover photographs: Marcy and Jerry Monkman, EcoPhotography
Cover design: Alicia Ozyjowski
Text design: Cathy Earl

Copyright © 1981, 1998 by Appalachian Mountain Club. All rights reserved.

Published by the Appalachian Mountain Club, 5 Joy St., Boston, MA 02108. Distributed by the Globe Pequot Press, 6 Business Park Rd., P.O. Box 833, Old Saybrook, CT 06475.

All rights reserved. No part of this publication may be reproduced or transmitted in any form or by any means, electronic or mechanical, including photocopying and recording, or by any information storage or retrieval system, except as may be expressly permitted by the 1976 Copyright Act or in writing from the publisher. Requests for permission should be addressed in writing to Appalachian Mountain Club Books, 5 Joy St., Boston, MA 02108.

THIRD EDITION

Library of Congress Cataloging-in-Publication Data
Demrow, Carl.
    The complete guide to trail building and maintenance / Carl
Demrow & David Salisbury. —3rd ed.
    p.   cm.
Includes index.
ISBN 1-878239-54-6 (alk. paper)
1. Trails—Design and construction. 2. Trails—Maintenance and
repair. I. Salisbury, David. II. Title.
TE304.D46   1998
625.7—dc21   98-9799
                                                        CIP

The paper used in this publication meets the minimum requirements of the American National Standard for Information Sciences—Permanence of Paper for Printed Library Materials, ANSI Z39.48–1984.∞

Due to changes in conditions, use of the information in this book is at the sole risk of the user.

Printed on recycled paper using soy-based inks.
Printed in the United States of America.

10 9 8 7 6 5 4 3 2 1   98 99 00 01 02 03 04

CONTENTS

CHAPTER ELEVEN
Developing and Using
Trail Maintenance Inventories   226

APPENDIX A

APPENDIX B

APPENDIX C

Introduction

It wasn't long ago that trail work consisted only of clearing the brush or blowdowns from the trail and keeping it blazed so people could find their way.

Times have changed.

Today, the most compelling reason for trail work is to conserve the fragile soils on which our trails are built and protect them from the never-ending onslaught of boots and water. Trail work in the present is not so much an exercise in clearing a path as it is an act of preserving our trails for the future.

This third edition presents trail work as an act of hands-on conservation, one that is designed to preserve soils, water quality, and vegetation. The philosophy of the AMC Trails Department is that trails are built and maintained to protect the environment, not to make passage through the woods easier (unless there is a safety issue involved). Bog bridges are used to preserve soils, vegetation, and water quality around the trail; they're not built simply to keep feet from becoming wet. Stone stairs harden the trail and stabilize soils; they aren't built to make the trip to the summit easier. All of the techniques discussed in this book are designed as much to protect the environment as they are to create enjoyable trails. This conservationist approach to trail building and maintenance helps bring to life the Appalachian Mountain Club's mission to promote the conservation and responsible use of the mountains, rivers, and forests of the Northeast.

Chapters 6 and 7, on materials for building and trail reconstruction, have been expanded and revised to include the new techniques that have been developed to aid in the conservation of trails and their soils over the past seventeen years. This edition stresses the need to maintain drainages as the most important element of trail maintenance in the Northeast. It details the use of rock over wood as a more durable and aesthetically sensitive material for trail building and reconstruction. This new edition also includes a chapter on safety and preparation. You'll find fifty new and revised illustrations and twenty-five new photographs. The chapters have been reordered to take you from preparation for trail work to laying out and building a trail, maintaining it, and reconstructing it.

Building on the methods chronicled in the first and second editions, this third edition crystallizes years of field experience and tried and true knowledge of the techniques that work best on the heavily used, easily eroded trails of the Northeast. Despite its roots in the Northeast, the information in this book can be used in almost any region of the country. The Appalachian Mountain Club's experience with trail building and maintenance dates back to the founding of the club in 1876. Today, the club's dedicated volunteers and staff maintain nearly 1,400 miles of trail from Washington, D.C. to Maine. Our trail program is dedicated to the protection and care of the trails and backcountry campsites of our region and the experiences they provide. We promote stewardship, public service, and ethical recreation.

Valuable to the novice and expert, this third edition covers everything from basic maintenance to the advanced skills of trail reconstruction and production of work logs. Terminology like "advanced skills" aside, none of what you'll find in this edition requires an advanced degree in environmental science or years of experience maintaining trails, so don't be intimidated. Finally, a guidebook cannot take the place of experience. Get in the field, learn firsthand, and give something back to the environment. You'll enjoy the experience and you'll have done your part to preserve our resources.

Acknowledgments

O f the many people involved in the publication of this book, two must be singled out as the inspiration for the third edition— Bob Proudman and Reuben Rajala. Their first and second editions of this book were groundbreaking in their time, and often were referred to by trail builders and maintainers as "the bible." The second edition in particular is the foundation on which this edition is built.

The AMC's trail crews deserve a hearty thanks for their innovative spirit and unceasing efforts to build a better mousetrap. The techniques, methods, and improvements reflected in this third edition have been developed and tested by AMC trail crews over the years.

There are many others who were involved in the production of this book who deserve thanks. Marcy and Jerry Monkman of EcoPhotography produced more than twenty-five new photos for the book, and Thomas and Jen Skehan of OffPiste Design worked closely and patiently with us to produce fifty new sketches for this edition.

Others assisted with the manuscript itself. Special thanks are owed to the following people: Jeanne Twehous and Vinny Spiotti for their assistance with chapter 1; Attorney Anne Dickenson Barber, who reviewed the section on landowner contact and liability and drafted portions of the chapter; David Tremblay of the Vermont Department of Agriculture provided supplemental text on soils; and Thom Perkins of Jackson Ski Touring Foundation reviewed and suggested changes to chapter 8. Kudos are also due Lester Kenway. Much of the material on the use of rigging and winches has been developed by Lester and generously imparted to the trail community over the years.

Our editor, Mark Russell, deserves extra special thanks for his patience, flexibility, counsel, hard work, and sense of humor. This edition would not have been possible without his most capable guidance.

Lastly, we wish to thank the AMC Books staff: Gordon Hardy for getting the project off the ground; Ola Frank for her wit, insight, and encouragement; and Elisabeth Brady for her always friendly answers to our always stupid questions.

Carl Demrow
David Salisbury
Pinkham Notch, N.H.
November 1997

CHAPTER ONE

Safety and Preparation: Work Safe, Work Smart

Trail work is satisfying, challenging, exhausting, frustrating, and fun, but it always has an element of danger. Cutting wood, digging ditches, and moving stones—the basics of trail work—are fraught with a hundred little perils and inconveniences, ranging from cuts, scrapes, and bruises to blisters, achy muscles, and dehydration. Any of these can temporarily affect how much you enjoy trail work and how much you can contribute. Ignore them for too long and they can keep you from your work altogether.

Other hazards are more threatening and require immediate attention. Hypothermia; heat stroke; injuries from tools, rocks, or falling trees; and similar serious conditions are usually due to minor mistakes or blunders that culminate in a major mishap. Following are five fundamentals of preparation that are essential for protecting you and your fellow trail workers when you head out to work on a trail.

- The Right Protective Gear
- The Right Food and Water
- The Right Work Plan and Tools
- The Right Training
- The Right Attitude

A trail worker's personal gear for a day of work in the mountains.

The Right Protective Gear

Boots and Socks

Good boots are the most important piece of gear any trail worker can have. A good pair of boots will get you into the work site comfortably and protect your feet while you work. Many people use lightweight cloth boots for hiking, but these boots provide minimal protection for work that involves moving large rocks or logs. If you are going to do a lot of trail work and can afford the steep price, buy yourself a pair of beefy all-leather hiking boots. They'll last a lot longer than the cloth boots and will protect your feet more; but be sure you break them in gradually before any long trips, to avoid blisters. Steel-toed boots will offer you an extra level of protection, but they are very uncomfortable for long hikes and have been known to make toenails fall off.

Help protect your feet from blistering with the right type of socks. Wear a light inner polypropylene liner to wick moisture away from your feet and reduce friction. For the outer sock, use a heavier-weight wool or wool blend. Don't wear cotton socks that will absorb moisture and increase the chance of blistering. As soon as you feel the onset of a blister or a hot spot, stop. Take your boots off, allow your feet to dry thoroughly, and apply moleskin, molefoam, or even duct tape to prevent further injury.

Gloves

Some people swear by gloves while others can't stand them. If your hands are callused and tough, you may prefer to work with bare hands. If you haven't recently done much manual labor, gloves will help prevent blisters on the pads below your fingers and on your thumbs. Gloves can also protect soft hands from the rough surfaces of rocks and tree bark, and can help keep pitch off your hands while debarking a tree. They can also protect against scratches from thorns and prickers. Leather gloves offer more protection than cotton gloves and are more durable. Use Kevlar gloves to protect your hands while you are operating a chain saw.

Eye Protection

Safety glasses are inexpensive and lightweight. Use the impact-resistant kind that offer protection on the sides as well as the front. While you don't need eye protection for all trail work, be sure to wear safety glasses during any ax work and all work involving hammers, chain saws, and the splitting or drilling of rocks. Remember, the mesh face protector on your chain-saw helmet does not provide sufficient eye protection.

Hard Hats and Chain-Saw Gear

Hard hats are a requirement in any area where there is potential danger from falling objects. Wear a hard hat when you work in an area with unstable rocks, when you fell trees, and when you work around standing trees with dead limbs (such limbs are

The right protective gear is essential for safer chain-saw operation.

known as widow makers for good reason).

Chain-saw safety is a whole book unto itself. The right protective gear is critical for safe chain-saw operation. Start with good, solid boots to protect your feet and insure good footing. If you are doing a lot of cutting and are concerned about footing, get a pair of caulked boots from a logging supply store. Caulked boots have short spikes protruding from the soles and will improve your footing, but are uncomfortable for hiking.

Chaps are required by both OSHA and good common sense. *Never* operate a chain saw without wearing a pair of chain-saw chaps. Chaps protect your legs with several layers of kevlar or padding that, if cut, will snag in the chain and stop it quickly. Most chain-saw injuries occur to the upper left thigh, so protect yourself by wearing a good pair of Underwriter's Laboratories (UL)–and American Pulpwood Association–rated chaps.

Eye guards, hearing protection, and hard hats also are required equipment for chain-saw use. The face mask on your hard hat does not count as eye protection. Get a good pair of impact-resistant goggles or safety glasses that meet ANSI Z87.1 specifications. Earmuffs that attach to your hard hat can be used for hearing protection. Or use foam plugs, if you find working with muffs too hot. Hard hats (either with or without face shields) and earmuffs are available from any logging equipment supplier. All forms of hearing protection have a Noise Reduction Rating (NRR) that specifies the number of decibels (dB) they reduce.

Kevlar gloves will offer you extra protection from a broken chain and other mishaps. Your chain saw also has built-in safety equipment. Do not use a chain saw without a chain brake, trigger lockout, rear hand guard, and vibration dampener.

In any type of felling work, the tree can kill or injure a person as fast as a chain saw can. Good training is critical to safe felling and chain-saw operation. See chapter 6 for more information on tree work and chapter 10 for more information on personal protective gear for chain-saw work.

Long Pants

Long pants are a matter of personal preference—some swear by them for protection from nicks and cuts, and others wouldn't think of wearing them because they are too hot in summer. There are certain of types of work—like log work, rock work, or heavy brushing in briars or thorns—where long pants can be particularly helpful, but they are awkward to wear while hiking and can make traveling to a work site unbearably hot. If you use long pants for trail work, try hiking to the work site in a lightweight pair of shorts. Pull on the long pants when you get to the site.

Rain Gear and Insulation

Protect yourself from the environment and sudden changes in weather with a good wool or pile sweater and rain gear. Bring rain gear and insulation appropriate for your location. For instance, a poncho and light sweater might be fine in a valley or flat location, but those working in alpine areas or above treeline should be prepared with full rainwear and windsuit, and insulation appropriate for a worst-case weather scenario. Such might require several layers of insulation and a warm hat and gloves, even in the summer.

First-Aid Kit and Other Considerations

Protect yourself from the elements with good rain gear, insulation, and other appropriate clothing.

Every trail crew, even a one-person crew, needs a first-aid kit. The contents should reflect the number of people in the crew, hazards posed by the work, and the remoteness of the work location. Inventory your first-aid kit regularly and replenish any used or damaged supplies. Suggested first-aid kit contents for a one-person crew and an eight-person crew are listed in appendices A and B.

Protect yourself from the local plant, insect, and animal life. If you are working in an area infested with poison ivy, poison oak, or other irritating plants, warn people ahead of time. Point out the plant, and in the case of poison oak, ivy, or sumac, have a bottle of Tecnu or a cake of Fels Naptha soap so exposed workers can wash off the irritating oil. The same applies for poisonous snakes; warn the crew, identify the species to avoid, and have a first-aid and evacuation plan should someone get bitten.

Insects can wreak havoc with a trail worker's sanity, and in extreme cases may produce an allergic reaction. Carry plenty of bug repellent. Anyone allergic to bees or other stinging insects should have his/her bee kit, and the crew member responsible for first aid should consider obtaining an epinephrine pen for medical emergencies involving anaphylactic shock. (Note: Epi pens and Ana kits can be obtained only with a prescription.)

The Right Food and Water

Stay properly hydrated—you'll be a safer, more efficient trail worker. Proper hydration will help you avoid environmental threats like hypothermia, heat exhaustion, and heat stroke. A dehydrated person will be sluggish and more susceptible to other injuries, and can have impaired judgment. Never head into the woods for a day of trail work with less than two quarts of water; bring more if it is hot and humid. Drink often rather than downing a quart in one sitting. Headaches are an indicator of dehydration, but the best indicator of hydration is urine. A properly hydrated person will have clear and copious urine.

Trail workers, like soldiers, run on their stomachs. Bring plenty of food with you and eat it—if you don't eat, you won't be able to work. Stick to a well-balanced diet with lots of carbohydrates. Some trail workers like their fats, but you'll need to drink extra water to burn off those fats. Don't skimp on food. If you are doing a lot of hard work, you'll need more food than you would for a day of sitting on the couch. Stick with food you know is healthy and will provide you with energy. Try to avoid caffeine and excessively salty foods that contribute to dehydration; and, stay away from large amounts of junk food or candy.

Plan on drinking at least *two quarts of water during the workday to stay minimally hydrated.*

The Right Work Plan and Tools

Plan and prepare your work ahead of time, and determine exactly which tools and how many of each you'll need. Know exactly what work you plan to do and where the work site is located. If need be, have the work site marked in advance of your trip. If you are leading a volunteer crew, it is especially important to mark your work ahead of time. It will minimize the amount of time the leader will need to orient him- or herself to the work, time that the volunteers are likely to be just standing around, waiting for someone to tell them what to do.

It is critically important that you bring the right tools, and enough of these tools, so that you and your crew can work effectively. There is no formula for this—you'll have to use your experience and judgment. Of course, don't hedge excessively and bring a lot of unneeded tools that will slow you down or make your crew doubt your leadership ability. The more you know about your work ahead of time, the better able you will be to select the right tools and the right amount. Avoid doing extra work that will require additional tools. Focus on one task, such as cleaning drainage, and bring only the tools you'll need for that job.

Set an attainable goal for the day—one that is ambitious but not out of reach. If you are leading a crew, tell them the goal in the morning and do your utmost to accomplish it. An example would be to clean all the drainages on a section of trail, or brush one mile of a trail, or install six rock steps. Having a goal will keep you focused and give you a sense of accomplishment at the end of the day.

The Right Training

Training has many different forms, but there are three things that every trail worker needs to know before receiving on-the-job training. Before you go into the woods on your first trip, you need to know how to lift heavy items safely, how to carry tools safely, and how to identify the Circle of Danger.

When lifting, pushing, or rolling, keep your back straight, your head up, and knees bent. Use the power of your legs (not your back) to move the object.

Lifting

Many trail workers have back problems because they failed to heed this simple advice—"Lift with your knees, not with your back!" Injuring your back will only cause endless hours of frustration and misery; severe injury may take you off the trail crew altogether.

A lot of trail work involves lifting everything from branches to logs, rocks, and tools. Trail work itself can give you a sore back, but lifting improperly can lead to serious problems. Always consider your back and how you can lessen the stress on it. When lifting, start with your knees bent, back straight, and feet shoulder-width apart. Keep your shoulders and neck straight. Lift the object gradually rather than jerk it up. If you are moving (pushing) a heavy object along the ground, keep your back straight and parallel with the direction you are pushing. Exert force on the object again with your knees.

Carrying Tools

There's a right way and a wrong way to carry tools. Whenever you carry a tool with sharp teeth, blade, point, or sharpened surface, carry the tool at your side with the sharp or pointed part away from you. Should you trip, stumble, or fall (and you will), simply toss the tool to your side to avoid injury to yourself or the person in front of or behind you. Give the person in front of you plenty of room, particularly if you are carrying a heavy rock bar or a tool with a sharp

point that you can't hold to your side. Use blade guards and sheaths, particularly when you are hiking in to or out of a work site. Switch hands often to avoid fatigue, and, if you can do it comfortably, use your pack to carry excess tools. Don't carry tools on your shoulder, where they can easily whack you in the head if you fall.

Carry all tools at your side with sharp edges or points down and away from your body.

Circle of Danger

The Circle of Danger is the area around the worker that is unsafe due to tool use. It surrounds anyone working with or even carrying a tool. The primary or inner Circle of Danger extends as far as the tool can reach while the worker is using it. The secondary outer Circle of Danger is the distance the tool could reach if the worker lost control or let go of the tool. The outer circle is particularly important with tools like axes and swizzle sticks, where the quick swinging motion of the tool spells danger when combined with a broken handle or a lost grip. Workers should never enter someone's primary Circle of Danger while he/she is working, and should never enter the outer circle in the direct path of a swing. The person using the tool must always be aware of those around him/her and ask others to move away if they are too close.

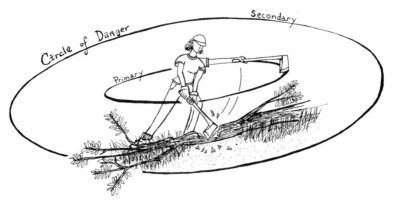

The tool user is responsible for his/her own Circle of Danger and the hazard it poses to others.

The Right Attitude

Now that you've got the right safety gear, food and water, work plan and tools, and training, you are almost ready to get to work. Before you set out on the trail, get in the right mind-set. Put safety first. When you have to make decisions, always err on the side of safety. Remember, there is no 911 in the woods; should you get hurt or injured, help may be a long time and far away. Serious injuries could prevent you from doing trail work in the future.

If you are leading crews, hold a quick meeting each morning before you work. Run through the five fundamentals of preparation. Make certain that everyone has the personal and safety gear needed and enough water. Go over the goals for the day and what you'll need for tools. Don't assign people to work they haven't been trained for, and instill the right attitude in your crew with a reminder to put safety first. Crew leaders, or even individuals, should always have an evacuation plan either in writing or in mind to use if needed. Leaders should monitor crew safety levels continually and should communicate with the crew if changes are needed. They should be doubly aware of their own behavior and practices, since their actions will set the tone with the crew.

Start the day by reviewing the five fundamentals of preparation with your crew.

The Next Step

The rest of your training will likely be on-the-job, but the AMC and many other trail clubs offer trail work training in subjects ranging from basic trail maintenance to chain-saw safety to rock work and crosscut-saw sharpening. Training with other trail workers is fun, increases your ability, and gives you an opportunity to ask questions about trail work. With many clubs, training is required for those who wish to adopt or maintain a section of trail on their own.

Leading crews is challenging and requires skills beyond basic trail work. If you want to lead crews, acquire first-aid certification and leadership training. First-aid training will give you an extra measure of risk management and is required for many leaders. Leadership training helps with the finer points of leadership, and you will likely find that you have "blind spots" in your leadership skills and abilities that you can improve upon. Leadership training is available from many different trail clubs and organizations, including the AMC.

Use common sense and go through the five fundamentals of preparation before you head out. Work safe and work smart. The trails and your fellow trail workers need you.

CHAPTER TWO
What Is a Trail?

"The job of recreational engineering is not one of building trails into lovely country, but of building receptivity into the yet unloving human mind."

—Aldo Leopold

Some believe that the primary purpose of trails is to provide access to a certain area or place. While trails do tend to provide links to other trails, features, or facilities, the value of a trail also lies in the journey it provides. That's why a trail should enhance the natural experience, not detract from it. *Webster's New World Dictionary* defines a trail as "a blazed or trodden path through a wild region." But it's more than that—a good trail also protects the region it passes through from damage by use and the forces of nature. Ultimately, a trail is a vehicle for the experience of travel through a natural area.

Trail Anatomy 101

A trail is made up of components, the sum of which make up the *trail landscape* or the environment seen by the hiker. These components complement each other in the hiker's experience of a trail.

All trails have *terminuses*, which are respectively the *trailhead* or start of the trail (usually at roadside) and the *destination*, be it a mountain summit, waterfall, mill site, or similar feature. Destinations in a system of trails will, for any single trail, include other trails and possibly campsites or other overnight facilities.

The *trail treadway* or *trail tread* is the surface upon which the hiker makes direct contact with the ground. It is the location for

The treadway *is the surface where the hiker makes direct contact with the ground.*

virtually all improvements intended to conserve soil resources. These improvements (which often also make hiking easier) usually involve the hardening and stabilizing of soils to prevent them from shifting, eroding, or becoming muddy. Popular trails in sensitive areas such as slopes and wet terrain will inevitably get damaged; therefore, good maintenance of the treadway occasionally requires reconstruction and rehabilitation of the original soil profile. The treadway is the most important component of any foot trail.

The trail *right of way* is the area around the treadway that is cleared for passage of the hiker. It is usually four to six feet wide, depending on vegetation density. If a trail has other uses besides hiking, such as cross-country skiing or mountain biking, the right of way will likely be wider. The term "right of way" also refers to legal right of passage, as would be the case with a protected trail on private land.

The *buffer* or *protective zone* is the land area on each side of the trail treadway. Buffer zones are the areas that lessen the impact on buffer zone

TREADWAY } right of way

buffer zone

Buffer zones insulate hikers...

the hiker from activities detrimental to the hiking experience, such as second-home development, mining, or logging. While the hiker may still hear, see, or even smell such activities, the buffer does provide some degree of mitigation for hikers and his/her experience.

Buffers can also be used to protect particularly fragile areas from hikers. Trail layout around sensitive plant life, lake shores, and springs should include buffers to protect these fragile areas from trampling.

The *trail corridor* includes the treadway, right of way, buffer zones, and all the lands that make up the environment of the trail as experienced by the hiker. The Forest Service has called it the "zone of travel influence." This terminology shows that the corridor

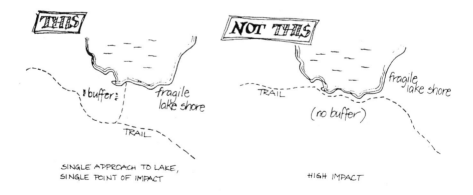

THIS

NOT THIS

buffer — fragile lake shore

TRAIL

TRAIL — fragile lake shore

(no buffer)

SINGLE APPROACH TO LAKE, SINGLE POINT OF IMPACT

HIGH IMPACT

...or insulate fragile areas from hiker impact.

The trail corridor *includes the treadway, right-of-way, buffer zones, and all the lands that make up the environment of the trail as experienced by the hiker.*

includes all those lands having an effect on the hiker's perception of the trail environment.

In particularly important trail systems, such as the Appalachian National Scenic Trail, this corridor takes on added importance. Legislation passed by the U.S. Congress requires that the corridor of the Appalachian Trail be protected from adverse developments that would be detrimental to its natural quality. Along virtually all of the Appalachian Trail, the trail and its zone of influence are protected by a 1,000-foot corridor, though in open forests, on lake shores, and above treeline this obviously does not include all the lands that influence the hiker.

Erosion Control

Erosion control covers virtually every type of improvement or alteration to the trail tread. Erosion control measures fall into four different categories that will be covered in chapter 6.

Drainage consists of devices or structures, such as water bars and drainage dips and ditches, that remove water from the trail tread or prevent water from getting on the tread. The purpose of drainage is to limit or eliminate the effects of erosion on the trail tread.

Stabilizers are used to hold soil in place and prevent erosion from water, feet, gravity, or other forces. Stabilizers include rock steps (used to stabilize steep gullied or eroding slopes) and cribbing (used to anchor soil above or below a trail on a slope).

Hardeners are used to eliminate the impact of foot travel through wet areas, and include bog bridges, step stones, and turnpiking, which involves constructing a raised tread.

Definers are used to channel or focus foot traffic onto a hardened or harder tread, thus protecting soils that may be wet, thin, or home to fragile plant life. Scree, often used in alpine zones or to define a rock staircase, is a good example. Rock steps are also considered definers.

These are broad categories, and elements of more than one category can be found in a water bar, bog bridge, or stone step. More importantly, all types of erosion control should be used in concert to provide a trail with its own, custom-made erosion control system.

Trail Formats

There are three major trail formats that can be combined to comprise a trail system.

The *loop* is a popular format for day-use trails because it enables easy access and parking. Hikers do not have to return on the same trail, thus maximizing hiker interest and satisfaction.

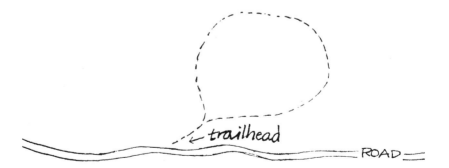

Loop

Horseshoe

The *horseshoe* can be a valuable trail format, especially in areas where public transportation is available. It can be used also as an appropriate alternative to auto travel on roads where distances between terminuses are not too great. Ski touring trail development in the Mount Washington Valley of New Hampshire has trailheads at inns and restaurants in the valley connected by trails in the horseshoe format. Many hiking trails are of this type.

The *line* is the simplest and most common format for trails. It connects two points—the roadside trailhead and the destination, which may be a summit, waterfall, or similar feature. A good example of trails in the line format are fire warden's trails to lookout towers on mountain summits. Long-distance trails such as the

Line

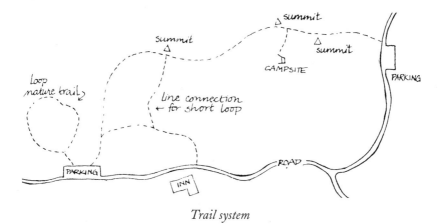

Trail system

Appalachian Trail and Pacific Crest Trail are prime examples of trails in the line format. These "trunk line" trails on public lands with high scenic value are augmented with side trails, alternate routes, and connectors to form trail systems.

A *trail system* can combine these different formats to satisfy a diversity of recreation needs. Careful design will provide trails for different users with different expectations. Multiday backpackers, day hikers, and others can be served by a well-designed trail system.

CHAPTER THREE
Trails on Private Land

Trail building in the East, where much of the land is privately owned, often involves constructing a trail on someone's property. In addition to the standard challenge of considering soils, topography, and vegetation, trail builders face the demanding and varied requirements of landowners as conditions for the use of their properties.

The benefits of creating trails on private land are fairly obvious. Greenway and suburban hiking and recreation paths, which increasingly cross private land, provide recreational opportunities close to home. Trails crossing private land provide enhanced access to town and county parks and offer recreational opportunities normally reserved for vacation times and landscapes farther afield. Local trails also enhance environmental education, and school curricula can often use the very development and maintenance of trails to enhance nature study. Finally, local trails can imbue the public with conservation and land-use values.

Despite these community benefits, landowners have legitimate concerns about allowing trails to be built on their land. Although most landowners are primarily concerned about liability and future use, there are other kinds of landowners and concerns. Use the information in this section to make your best effort at securing the best possible level of future protection for your trail.

Determining Ownerships in a Proposed Trail Corridor

Once you've documented trail needs and decided to proceed with the construction of your trail, you'll need to investigate ownership of the land along your proposed trail corridor. In order to maintain flexibility for negotiations with owners, your initial stages of planning should include a broad trail corridor including alternate trail locations. Inflexible trail plans that rely on one key parcel of privately held land can be foiled if that owner refuses to cooperate.

Steps for researching landowners:

1. *Obtain access to town tax maps (if they exist).* Such maps are usually kept by the assessor's office or the town clerk. The maps are public information and are available for anyone to examine. The information is quite complete, although the boundary lines are not always accurate and do not claim to be so. The maps are usually cross-referenced with owners' names and addresses; they also indicate acreage and may indicate the existing easements and right of ways across properties.

2. *Research deeds in the county registry of deeds.* In addition to checking names and addresses, it is important to look for any easements or restrictions which might already apply to the property. If the town has no tax maps, the process is far more complex, a bit like solving a jigsaw puzzle. Here are some suggestions:

   • Get to know the locals. Local residents are probably the most useful sources of information because they are familiar with the use of land over time, attitudes toward conservation, financial status of individual owners, and future plans for the region. Ask local residents who are sympathetic to the trail project for general landownership, patterns, specific owners (if known), and ideas on who would be most favorably inclined toward the idea of a trail and land preservation. Find out who else would know landowners and, if necessary, ask for an introduction.

- Talk to town selectmen. If supportive of the proposed trail, they can be a good source of information, often knowing from memory who owns what land. The selectmen's office should have complete lists of property owners together with acreage, addresses, and taxes paid. (However, they may have not have boundary maps.) They also can give an idea of how much land is being sold in the town, what the various land uses are, and what future plans might affect the trail. Maintain a good working relationship with the town selectmen, as they may be useful when actually talking with landowners; in very small towns, their opinions may carry a great deal of weight.

- Talk with surveyors who have surveyed land in the area. Often, a few surveyors have been working a region for a number of years and know the land and landowners well, particularly with regard to the larger landholdings. They are a good source of information on existing woods roads, current use of the land, and outstanding natural features. Sympathetic surveyors who have good relations with landowners and the town can often act as references when you call on landowners.

- Check with conservation officers of state fish and game departments, county foresters, and consultants from the USDA Natural Resource Conservation Service. Often they know a particular area well and can recommend certain landowners who would be more favorably inclined to the project than others. Their greatest help, however, is in knowing the land and its features.

- The chairpersons of town conservation commissions are extremely helpful in most cases, especially since they are aware of the prevalent conservation attitudes in the town. Again, they can be most useful when actually contacting landowners.

Types and Patterns of Ownership

The types and patterns of landownership play an important role in the design and layout of a trail. Studying overall types and patterns of landownership will help to determine which landowners are most approachable and, by extension, where it is easiest and most economical to lay a trail.

Corporate Owners: Pulp and Paper Companies, Agricultural Ownerships

Lands held by corporations for timber harvesting and agriculture can be ideal for trail use. Well-planned trail use can be easily adapted to the management programs of these ownerships and provide an opportunity for the owners to communicate their management values to the public, and negotiations with one corporate owner often can yield access to large tracts of land. These agricultural lands are not disrupted by trail use in the same way residential land would be. Hikers are less bothersome to absentee owners than they are to residential owners who experience the use of their land firsthand.

However, corporate owners tend to have some very specific concerns. Before you approach these owners with a trail proposal, develop your vision in a manner that acknowledges their concerns. These concerns generally are oriented around how the trail will affect future use of the land. Enthusiastic use by the public would make trail closure a bad public relations issue; however, corporate decisions tend to be based on financial gain or loss and not hiker satisfaction. Accidents could pose an unacceptable liability burden to the corporate owner; also, the very real concerns of fire hazard, parking congestion, vandalism, and sanitation problems can make obtaining endorsement of trail proposals by these owners difficult.

Corporate Owners: Developers and Subdividers

Owners whose purpose is to develop their landholdings are most often negative about proposals for trail use. From their viewpoint, trails unrealistically foreclose their options (though some developers may see the presence of recreational trail on their land as a potential selling point).

Designating land for development virtually precludes the possibility of high-quality trail design because such land tends to be subdivided into small units. There have been many cases where existing trails were closed because access had been cut off by development. Many informal, unmaintained paths around cities and towns have been effectively closed in recent years by urban sprawl, such as limited-access highways, airports, and the like. Land held for development presents only limited trail options and narrows the possibility of successful public trail use.

Residential Owners

In town and near urban centers, most ownerships are residential (i.e., owners live on or close to their property). These ownerships require closer, more thorough follow-up for trail installation. Owner attitudes are varied and, in order to meet these varied perspectives, trail design necessarily becomes more complex.

A conservation-minded owner will be easier to negotiate with because he or she shares and can understand the social and environmental goals of the proposed trail. Document owner attitudes during initial research wherever possible. This way, further negotiations can be facilitated by approaching the most sympathetic owners first. The endorsement from these owners will help their less sympathetic neighbors to accept the idea of public trail use. Depending on the situation, protection of trails on residential land can be so complex as to be unrealistic for trail projects.

Talking to the Landowners

The development and utilization of land protection devices for trail corridors is still in the early stages of development. It is a vast subject that at some stage usually requires legal counsel, considerable expenses, and time-consuming negotiations. This book contains only a cursory review of some of the available mechanisms and their benefits and drawbacks when applied to trail development.

Crystal-clear communication is essential. All parties involved must clearly understand the goals of the trail project, how they will be accomplished, and what role each party will play or how the project will affect them. If policies and modes of implementation are not clearly understood and collectively acknowledged, then negotiations for agreements aren't likely to be successful.

Tact and enthusiasm are critical for the person carrying out the negotiations with owners, and a good public relations profile in the proposed trail region helps pave the way to the owner's door. In public relations, the policies underlying implementation of the project must be clearly understood. Conflicting information sows seeds of distrust and reticence in landowners. Develop a solid vision with a flexible plan before you talk to landowners.

Many landowners feel defensive about their rights, so use a low-key, soft-sell approach to reduce the likelihood that an owner will feel threatened. This is especially important today, when demands on the private sector are growing. Despite the need for a soft-sell approach, you'll need to be firm. Legal agreements that do not bind the owner to conditions that perpetuate a high-quality environment for the trail don't supply the protection that trails desperately need. A legal agreement must sustain and preserve the trail for long periods of time and throughout changes in landownership in order for the trail to be successful.

Your negotiator must be thoroughly familiar with the characteristics of the land on which the trail is proposed. Before approaching an owner, the negotiator should have information on the owner's perspectives and views on trail use that will help the negotiator develop a successful pitch and a proposal that best suits the landowner's individual needs. Although individual adaptations of the trail arrangement for each owner can be made, every owner should feel as though he or she is being treated equally. Mistrust can develop among neighboring owners if special accommodations are made for one particular owner.

Different Forms of Trail Protection

There are five legal arrangements that can establish a trail right of way: oral agreements, easements, leases, licenses, and land acquisitions. Between the two extremes of oral agreement and a complete transfer of ownership there are three limited legal interests that can be placed on trail corridor land. These nonpossessory interests in land offer much flexibility and are excellent techniques for realizing private wishes with respect to the land. In order to protect a trail and its corridor, the goal is to use the arrangement the landowner finds agreeable and which provides the longest protection to the trail and is the most binding. Any legal arrangement requires careful consideration of its respective characteristics.

Oral Agreements

Generally a contract involving the sale of real estate is not binding unless it is in writing. An oral agreement that actually transfers ownership of land is not legally binding. Although some types of agreements for the use of land do not need to be in writing, an oral agreement will always be difficult to enforce because the parties may disagree over the original terms of their contract. An oral agreement is, therefore, inappropriate for use in a trail project except during the preliminary planning stages.

Ownership-in-Fee

Ownership-in-fee is a complete transfer of ownership from landowner to trail steward. Ownership-in-fee may not be financially feasible, or necessary, except perhaps where permanent facilities such as parking lots and campsites are provided. Depending on how sophisticated your negotiator is, however, a landowner may have tax or estate planning concerns which make his or her donation of land to a nonprofit concern appealing. This may be something to explore with the landowner.

Easement

The easement is the strongest of the nonpossessory interests in land. An easement grants a nonowner the right to use a specific portion of the land for a specific purpose. The extent of the interest conveyed needs to be explicitly outlined in the deed of conveyance, which is recorded in public records of title. An easement may be limited to a specific period of time or may be granted in perpetuity; or, the termination of the easement may be predicated upon the occurrence of a specific event (for example, "so long as the bridge is maintained" or "unless and until the property is zoned for commercial development"). An easement agreement "runs with the land," meaning it survives transfer of landownership and is generally binding upon future owners until it expires on its own terms.

Lease

The lease involves the granting of an interest in land upon the payment of an agreed-upon fee. The fee does not have to be monetary, but some consideration must be given for the right to use the land or the lease will not be legally binding. A lease agreement has the advantage to the landowner of being a terminable arrangement upon the expiration of a certain period of time, but the power of termination is limited to the terms of the written arrangement.

License

The most limited nonpossessory interest in land is the license, which is revocable at the will of either party to the agreement. Unlike an easement, a license does not run with the land, and the death of the licensor generally will terminate the license. The license simply permits the licensed party to enter the land of the licensor without being deemed a trespasser. In general, the license does not have to be in writing to be legally binding. The license is the simplest legal device and the least formidable to the owner, who will be assured that there is no threat of litigation should he or she decide that the arrangement is no longer in his or her best interest. The nonbinding character of the license makes it fairly easy to consummate with owners; however, it has obvious limitations as a device to secure land for trails.

When negotiating a right of way for a trail, it is important to include an agreement as to whether and how the landowner can use the right of way. In this way, the trail can be kept free of unnecessary obstacles and encroachments. Some minimum distance around the trail must also be kept free of incompatible developments and aesthetic concerns such as highways, structures, and timber-harvesting activity. The easement provided for the trail corridor can be from eight feet to a quarter of a mile depending on the owner, the financial resources of the trail sponsor, and the vision for the proposed trail.

Concerns of Private Landowners

A legally binding agreement may require a commitment too great for an owner to accept. Keep in mind that the freedom to make decisions about property is a highly valued right and is constitutionally guaranteed.

Owner concerns regarding public trail development and any accompanying proposed legally binding arrangement are entirely legitimate. To see a trail proposal from the owner's perspective, consider the following points:

Future Use of the Proposed Trail Property

The major concern for protecting trail rights of way or easements are the landowner's future right to use property proposed for the trail. Trails need not be protected with legal agreements, but without some protection a trail's future cannot be securely guaranteed.

Try to anticipate the owner's reaction so that the trail proposal does not sound unreasonable. The trail sponsor must enter negotiations with a firm sense of the owner's attitude. In initial transactions, it may be best simply to secure a written pledge from the owner to continue to work with the trail sponsor toward installation and eventual protection.

Trails, because of their linear nature, can easily bisect property into compartments, which can place a serious constraint on the property's use. The right-of-way agreement should permit motorized crossing of the corridor and possibly limited use of vehicles along the trail treadway. This concession, plus the latitude to cut timber according to a simple prescription, offers the possibility of some protection to the trail while giving the owner essential freedom in the management of his or her lands.

On a trail route for which no alternatives exist, you'll need to adapt the agreement to the owner's conditions. Sometimes the owner's plans may preclude trail development altogether. If this is the case, nothing can be done to change the situation and alternative trail routes must be found. Remember, the less commitment that is required from landowners, the easier the sales job.

In some cases, the best course of action may be to begin simply by getting verbal or written permission from the owner to build the trail. This approach may work well with reticent owners. If installation of the trail proceeds with little trouble to the landowner, and maintenance work is top-notch, the landowner may be won over and may be willing to allow increasingly more trail-protective agreements. Unfortunately, in this litigious and suspicious world, obtaining verbal permission for trail use may not be effective in actually protecting the trail. The tenuous status of most trails on private land must be fortified with viable agreements to protect and perpetuate these facilities. If trails are not protected, developments will continue to reduce our hiking opportunities.

Liability for Hiker Injury and Costs of Legal Self-Defense

Landowners are frequently concerned that if they give approval to the proposed trail, they are tacitly accepting liability for accidents that hikers may have on their property. Landowners fear that their failure to provide hikers with warnings about dangerous conditions on the land, or their failure to inspect trails regularly and draw attention to possible hazards on the trail, will result in a lawsuit by an injured hiker against the landowner. These lawsuits are usually based on an argument that the landowner has been legally negligent by failing to protect the hiker from hazards even though the landowner knew that the hiker was going to use his or her land. In order to establish that a landowner has been legally negligent, the person who is bringing legal action (the plaintiff) must prove four elements:

Duty

The plaintiff must prove that the landowner had some obligation or duty recognized by law to protect the plaintiff from unreasonable risk. In law, there is a standard of conduct by which the actions of the landowner are judged. For example, if landowners in general prune dead branches off trees that overhang a public walkway in order to make the walkway safe, a landowner who does not do so would not have lived up to the legal standard of conduct for landowners and might be liable for the injuries of a hiker who gets hit by a dead branch while using the walkway.

Breach

The failure on the owner's part to conform to the standard of conduct that the law requires is considered a breach. In the previous scenario, the landowner has not pruned the branches on the tree and therefore he has breached his duty to do so.

Proximate Cause

The plaintiff must also establish a reasonably close causal connection between the conduct and the resulting injury. In the same example, the landowner's neglect of the tree was the actual cause of the dead branch remaining on the tree until it fell off and hit the passerby. There is a direct relationship between the landowner's actions (or inactions) and the harm to the hiker.

Damage

The action or inaction of the negligent party must result in actual quantifiable loss or damage to the injured party. Following the same example, the hiker only has a cause of action if he is injured by the falling tree limb. If the hiker sustains a head wound and has to be rushed to the hospital, he has been damaged. If the branch startles him and he is annoyed or momentarily frightened by the fact that it fell, no actual injury has occurred and he cannot recover for the landowner's actions.

Burden of Proof

The burden of proof in a lawsuit for negligence is on the injured party. This means that the injured party must prove each element of his or her case by a preponderance of the evidence. The defendant landowner, however, must still pay for a legal defense. Even though landowner liability is often limited by state recreational-use statutes, these statutes do not eliminate the right to sue. In our lawsuit-ridden society, defending yourself against even a frivolous lawsuit can spell financial ruin. Landowners have a legitimate concern over the cost of self-defense, even though few, if any, cases have resulted in serious financial peril.

Extent of Duty

Identifying the extent of the duty that the landowner has to the hiker is important because, as indicated in the outline of requirements for negligence, landowner liability is predicated upon the breach of the duty owed to another person. The extent of the duty owed by a landowner to users of his land depends on the legal status of the person using the land.

Case Law

In some states, the law provides for categories of persons entitled to use land, and establishes a hierarchy of land users, most generally called trespassers, licensees, and invitees. Most states have abolished this hierarchy, and focus instead on whether the landowner's conduct toward a person on his land is reasonable. Some discussion of the different categories is useful to demonstrate what "reasonable" treatment by the landlord might be.

A "trespasser" enters the landowner's property intentionally and without privilege or consent of the landowner. The landowner owes no duty to the trespasser to use reasonable care to keep his lands safe for the trespasser; however, the landowner may not set traps for the trespasser. If the landowner knows of the trespasser's existence, the landowner has a duty to warn the trespasser of conditions on the land that are serious or life threatening.

A landowner may have an additional duty to trespassing children, because children are immature and cannot accurately judge the degree of risk as an adult can. This is particularly true when the landowner knows that children are trespassing, in which case he has a more heightened duty to protect them from dangers on his land. Thus the law does not think it reasonable conduct on the part of the landowner to leave unsecured dangerous equipment where children might play, or fail to warn of thin ice on a pond if he knows children often skate on the pond and he knows that the ice is thin.

To "licensees," people who have been given permission to use land but who do so for their own reasons and with no benefit to the landowner, the landowner owes a greater duty. The landowner does not need to inspect his property for safety, nor does he have to warn of hazards that should be obvious to the licensee. The landowner owes the greatest amount of duty to "invitees," people who are invited by the owner to enter the property at some benefit to the owner, be it social, financial, or otherwise. The landowner must protect the invitee from known hazards, but the landowner has an affirmative duty to protect the invitee against hazards that he or she, with reasonable care, might discover in exploring the land.

The reasonableness test does not really make a clear distinction between the licensee and the invitee but instead examines the landowner's conduct. The court looks at what a particular person was doing on the land, and what that person could reasonably have expected from the landowner. For example, if the landowner lets people fish in his pond, he may only have a duty to warn them of known dangers. But if he suspects that the bank of the pond is eroding and is unsafe, the court may determine that the landowner had a duty to check the bank of the pond and ensure that the fishermen were safe.

Opening land to the public implies that it has been prepared for their reception. It seems clear that the hiker should accept the risks of her activities as her own. However, to date, the legal duty owed to a hiker has not been established clearly, and no determination would cover every circumstance. It seems likely that the courts will enforce greater responsibility on owners in the future because of a generally increasing concern for safety, as evident in the consumer movement and other such trends in our society.

Statutory Law

Many states have recreational-use statutes that limit the liability of owners who allow the public to use their lands for recreational purposes such as hiking, skiing, or mountain biking. Generally, these laws protect only landowners who permit use of their lands without charge. The statutes may also provide a specific level of care below which the landowner is liable. These laws help to minimize the duty of landowners toward recreational land users, thereby encouraging landowners to allow the recreational use of their land. These statutes also serve to keep liability insurance premiums at a fairly low cost, which consequently makes it feasible for landowners to purchase insurance to protect themselves when they open their lands to recreational use. While these laws limit liability, they do not eliminate the threat of lawsuits or the legal burden of self-defense. So, landowners do have a legitimate concern over the cost they may incur defending against a frivolous or malicious lawsuit.

Indemnifications

Indemnification of landowners by the responsible trail club is one way to alleviate the very real concern over liability. Indemnification should only be done on a case-by-case basis, and then only after the trail club has obtained a qualified legal opinion.

Insurance spreads risk over a population large enough so that no insured party would suffer unacceptable losses in the event of a mishap. Insurance is available to private landowners concerned with the liability they may incur by opening land to hiking. Most landowners have homeowner's insurance policies that adequately cover their risks. However, if the landowner lacks insurance, or if additional coverage is deemed necessary, it might best be purchased by the trail sponsor, with the landowner as the beneficiary.

When seeking proper insurance, a local agent usually knows best a landowner's needs. It is important that this agent understand the nature of the recreational program as well as the volume of recreational use and potential hazards. State laws limiting landowner liability should be brought to the attention of the agent.

Because the insurance market for private recreation facilities is relatively new, it benefits the trail sponsor or owner to seek rates from several companies before making a final choice. Liability insurance covers losses suffered by the owner as a result of a successful lawsuit by an injured hiker up to policy limits. The policy may cover expenses for medical treatment and rescue at the scene of the mishap. It may also cover investigation, defense, and settlement costs.

Sponsors

There are two basic types of liability insurance policies available to managers (sponsors) of recreation facilities on private land: the Owner, Landlord, and Tenant policy (OL&T) and the Comprehensive General Liability policy. If at all possible, policies should be reviewed by someone familiar with insurance terms and definitions in order to determine the actual extent of the coverage.

The OL&T policy is the basic method for covering legal liability to the public. Campgrounds and parking areas may be covered under this type of policy. In the past, many insurance companies have recommended coverage limits of $25,000 per person, $50,000 per accident, and $10,000 in property damages (25/50/10), but because of the increasing amount of court awards and liability claim settlements, higher limits should be considered.

The Comprehensive General Liability Policy offers extensive coverage unless specific risks are excluded. Its major advantage for trail use is that it covers almost all hazards.

Overuse, Vandalism, Parking, and Other Management Problems

If the owner's reservations regarding future use and liability are quelled, concerns over the actual management of the proposed trail may become the greatest cause for reticence in an owner's support. All of the problems that can develop on public trails can develop on trails in the private sector. These problems range from physical deterioration of soils through erosion to the social problems of over-crowding, vandalism, parking congestion, and littering. These problems and their attendant solutions are described in other parts of this book. A responsible trail organization will convince owners that problems have solutions and that these problems can be controlled by effective management.

The basic point, then, is to impart knowledge to the owner and inspire trust for the maintenance organization that will be responsible for the trail. It is presumed that the sponsoring organization will have made judgments on its own capability to meet this responsibility. This is imperative before winning landowner support; if management tasks exceed capabilities and problems develop, the owner's trust in the organization will be diminished.

A safe procedure for new trails is to limit information on the trail's availability and allow traffic to increase gradually. Management problems are almost directly proportional to the volume of use a trail receives. The capability of the maintaining organization will obviously not be as heavily taxed on a trail with low or moderate public use. If the information on a trail is limited, then so is use. Gradually increasing access to information on a trail serves to gradually increase the number of hikers on the trail. This gives the trail manager the staggered start he or she needs to develop a management style to support the higher profile that comes with increasing use. In this way problems can be solved earlier and not after they become full-blown irritants to the landowner.

CHAPTER FOUR

New Trail Layout and Construction

While none of the principles covered in this book constitute rocket science, there are many factors that trail maintainers must first carefully consider before they start cutting brush, putting up trail markings, and digging in the dirt. New trail building has four major phases: visioning, planning, layout, and construction. Visioning starts with the big picture, and each successive phase narrows in on the on-the-ground details. Good planning is arguably the single most important factor in a trail's success or failure, and can help to ensure that a trail is pleasant to its users and lies on the land as lightly as possible. Before you plan, you must first figure out what you are planning for.

Visioning

The visioning process focuses your thoughts about the trail you're trying to build. A good starting point is to ask the same questions a newspaper reporter asks when writing a story: who, when, where, and why.

- **Who** will use the trail, build it, maintain it, support it, manage it?

- **When** will it be built and used?

- **Where** will it go?

- **Why** is it necessary?

While there are many questions to consider, careful thinking will save you many headaches later on. For example, if you decide to build a trail for hikers and equestrians, you'll need to carefully consider how you are going to construct any bridges you may need (horses like wide bridges with rails), and how you will deal with any moist areas (areas that are fine for a few hikers' feet will turn into a morass after several horses pass by).

Building a trail by yourself is not recommended, unless you are a private landowner building a relatively short and simple trail on your own land. Form a group, a committee, or a loose association that can use the experience, skills, and judgment of several people to approach all angles of the trail. You'll make better decisions, avoid burnout, have more people to do all the dirty work, and enjoy the experience much more.

If you don't know the area that you are considering for a trail, research it. Find some maps and study local features. Walk the route in the woods and imagine where you generally might like the trail to go. Sketch the trail on a map, remembering that it will likely change as you begin to put the pieces together and deal with on-the-ground realities in successive phases. Learn the topography of the area. This sort of information gathering will be of great benefit later on in the process.

What is your trail going to look like? Keep these ideas in mind as you design your trail:

- Clearing and marking should be consistent along the trail to avoid confusion.

- Establish a plan for trail standards and stick to it.

- Avoid unnecessary loss of elevation where the trail climbs a slope. Hikers should not have to lose significant elevation unnecessarily because of poor design. A trail built to ascend into the high country or any significant slope should be consistent in this respect.

- Remember that hikers always look forward to a scenic vista. If you can't bring the main trail to a vista, then a side trail to the view will do the trick.

Take advantage of the natural curiosity hikers have for cultural and historic points of interest—like old dam and mill sites, cellar holes, and old villages. These places add value to a trail. Before you lay out your trail, do some research on the historical and cultural features of the area, and if possible, make them a part of your trail. Talk with the local historical society and involve them in the process. Include a brief description of such attractions in any interpretive information or guidebooks to maximize the benefit for users.

Sometimes the reputation of a feature—like a mountain summit, village site, or old mine—is enough to attract use even though a trail does not exist. In these cases a well-planned trail may be best to manage and concentrate foot traffic. For example, with enough use, trailless summits can be damaged by hikers who visit via bushwhacking or "bootleg" trails. Over time, some of these bootleg or unplanned trails are created just by continuous use and can approach a trailless summit like the spokes of a wheel approaching the hub. Providing access with a well-designed trail can prevent damage from such unmanaged de facto trails.

Your trail vision should take shape after you consider these factors. High-quality trail design is a balance between beauty and function, as natural features and scenery (outlooks, rock outcrops, and streams) are creatively juxtaposed with the continuity, efficiency, and durability of a proposed route. Your choice of route from beginning to end, plus your intended users, marking standards, and the natural character of the terrain and its features will define your trail. After creating your trail vision, you can anticipate all of the potential on-the-ground problems in the planning phase.

Planning

Anyone can scratch out a trail route on a map, but in the end a well thought out plan will make a successful trail. The planning phase's purpose is to anticipate every possible problem on all sections and areas of the trail and prevent them through design and corrective or preventative action. Start where your trails starts—the proposed parking area or trailhead—and mentally walk through the trail to anticipate potential problems you might encounter.

To help you identify the full scope of issues you'll need to eventually consider, look over some management plans for different trails, then sketch out your group's policy on some of those issues. For instance:

- How will you plan for search-and-rescue situations?

- What about overnight camping, wood fires, and water sources?

- Will you do community outreach?

- How will you manage large groups that use the trail?

- Will there be sanitary facilities?

- How will you prevent and respond to litter, graffiti, and vandalism?

- Will you have a leash policy for dogs?

- What will you do if a communication tower is proposed for a peak on your trail?

This book only covers issues relevant to trail building and maintenance, but we strongly advise that you become familiar with the wide range of potential trail issues.

Trailhead and Parking Facilities

The location of trailhead and parking facilities needs to be studied carefully in the planning phase. If a trailhead is proposed on a major recreational highway, visitor use will be high, so your trail standards must be correspondingly higher to protect the resources of the proposed trail corridor and hiker safety. Depending on the number of users and the soil conditions, the trail may need to be wider, hardened with rock "paving" or even bridging, and fortified with extra erosion-control devices to accommodate many users. Planning must be more comprehensive, and design and construction must be substantial if the trail is to be safe, enjoyable, and environmentally stable.

The location and size of parking facilities allow a degree of use control. If the designer wants a low volume of use, parking should be nonexistent or limited. If parking is plentiful and accessible, use may tend to be high, increasing the maintenance needs of the trail.

Parking facilities can be the most problematic part of a trail, so be certain to involve abutting landowners, local businesses, and the appropriate governmental agencies in the planning. For safety, the location of parking facilities on highways must be carefully planned and must be coordinated with the appropriate representatives of the state's highway department or department of transportation. Their specifications for the location of a parking facility on a highway will likely determine the location of the trailhead.

Coordinate parking facilities with other recreational uses. Use an existing picnic area for your trailhead to eliminate the need for a new parking lot. If a snowmobile trail has a parking area, then a summer hiking trail placed in the same vicinity will eliminate the cost of building additional facilities.

Place a signboard or kiosk at your trailhead to provide the hiker with rules and regulations, management information, maps, and other important information about the trail. Prevent vandalism by locating the signboard out of sight of the road and/or fifty feet in on the trail. Trailhead management can prevent other problems with litter and human waste; remember that some preventative educational efforts are much cheaper than new facilities. If you do need a more "developed" trailhead, plan your facilities carefully to avoid problems after installation.

Roads and Private Lands

Buffer the hiker from the sight and sounds of man-made features such as roads, railroad tracks, industrial zones, logging operations, and residential developments. In cases where the trail must cross a road, railroad, logging operation, or similar feature, place the trail to minimize hiker exposure and cross these areas in the shortest practical manner, preferably at right angles. Right-angle crossings are also safer for road and railroad crossings.

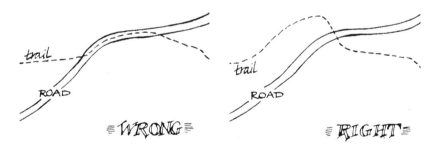

Design trails to cross roads at a perpendicular angle with good lines of sight.

When a trail crosses private land, acknowledge the generosity of the landowner with a special sign or mention in a brochure, and be sure to insist that trail users respect the private land they are using.

Long lines of sight should be avoided to keep conflicts with landowners to a minimum. If your trail crosses the property of a large paper or timber company owner, use the trail as an opportunity to educate hikers about timber management and the partnership you have with the corporate owner.

Topography

Variations in topography such as hills, knolls, and views are elements of a stimulating and interesting trail design. Fit the trail to the lay of the land so hikers will have a greater sense of adventure and anticipation in traveling. Use subtle turns and undulations in grade steepness, dramatic climbs to a view, or the sudden appearance of a waterfall to provide hikers with an interesting and satisfying hike.

Managing topography is very important when it comes to creating a trail with minimum environmental impact. Gullies caused by trail erosion will soon develop on trails that ascend long, steep gradients, so you must locate a happy medium between the trail's function of gaining elevation and the tendency of water and foot traffic to rapidly erode trails on steep grades. This happy medium can be found with a sidehill trail location; running water will cross the trail but not run down the treadway at high velocities that aggravate erosion. You can also break up steep climbs with short-level or sidehill stretches that provide low spots that allow natural drainage.

Switchbacks

To climb a long, steep grade on a mountain, a sidehill trail alone cannot provide the needed rise in elevation. The lateral area available for a sidehill trail is limited by terrain, so the trail must turn and start its lateral motion in the opposite direction. This turn is aptly named a "switchback." It has been used for centuries in road and trail design.

Basic switchback

On a well-designed trail, one switchback leg is not visible from another. Natural topographic features and the length of trail segments are varied to sustain interest. Remember, steady grades give the hiker a feeling of substantial progress when climbing.

Switchbacks that drain properly are difficult to build, so use long stretches between switchbacks. Minimize them to avoid the monotonous repetition they create and to hold initial construction costs and maintenance costs to manageable levels.

Switchbacks often fail when their upper and lower legs are built within view of each other. Hikers on a trail with closely spaced switchbacks will take shortcuts, especially when descending. Watercourses and erosion will develop on such shortcuts after they become trampled by large numbers of hikers.

Control shortcutting on switchbacks by using a wide turn. You may have to run a small section of the turn straight up the fall line, but if the danger of shortcutting is great, as is the case in open hardwoods or above treeline where hikers can see great distances, then a wide turn running straight up the grade may be the best choice to make. Harden the trail treadway on the steepest part of the turn with steps to keep the turn stable and durable.

Whenever possible, use natural features such as rock outcrops and dense stands of vegetation as shortcut barriers by placing them on the inside of a switchback. A view on the outer edge of a turn

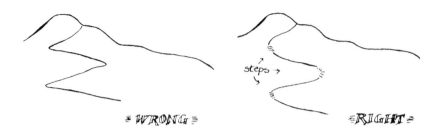

Narrow switchbacks lead to shortcutting; wide turns fortified with steps help prevent shortcutting.

can prove useful, for it can attract hiker attention to the corner instead of any shortcutting possibilities. Clearly mark switchbacks and abrupt changes in route direction to prevent hikers from walking off the trail at a turn.

Avoid building switchbacks on short, frequently used trails, such as between a water supply and a campsite, or a parking lot and a view. Switchbacks need a large area and adequate vegetative screening between legs. Short trails do not cover enough space to permit the proper design of foolproof switchbacks.

Rocks, cliffs, ledges, and caves provide points of interest along a trail. Don't avoid these rigors of the landscape when you design a trail; use caution when placing trails over shale slides, talus slopes, or cliff edges. Tree scars and talus with recently fractured surfaces indicate falling rock. It would be unreasonably dangerous to locate trails under these ledges and cliffs. Clearly define trails skirting the tops of cliffs. Recognize wet, mossy rock and ice in the spring and fall as dangerous in any cliffside location, and avoid them. If these limiting conditions are not serious, the trail should take every advantage of dramatic topography.

Be conscious of and avoid areas with evidence of landslides and rock slides. Avoid any area with evidence of avalanches if the trail is used in winter. All such areas may be prone to severe soil and vegetation movement or damage and can be hazardous to hikers.

You'll need a quick lesson in soil science to help you limit the trail's impact.

Soil Science for the Trail Planner 101

Trail planners must pay close attention to soil characteristics and how different types of soils respond to foot traffic. All aspects of soil are important to the trail planner, often because the planner must work with the existing soil. If you want to hike to the top of a high mountain, you will likely have to deal with a delicate alpine mor. Or, if you want people to experience a bog, you will be dealing with a devolved mull. If it's the seashore, expect peripatetic sand. The soil is also an important yet subtle part of the outdoor experience—just as critical as the flora, fauna, fresh air, and vistas. The clump of soil from the lug of a hiking boot left on a kitchen floor provides an important link to the natural world and the most recent hike.

Soil is a complex mix of minerals, organic matter, organisms, pore space, and water. It comprises the root zone of living plants. It is the product of climate and organisms acting, destructively and synthetically through time, on rocks.

Soil thickness varies—some areas have no soil, others have many feet of it. The soil mantle is like a mosaic, and it changes in relation to its parent materials. The soil found in a given area from the ground to bedrock is called the *soil profile*. Each soil profile is composed of layers (sometimes very small or "thin"). Your local USDA Natural Resource Conservation Service office or Agricultural Extension office will have detailed soil maps that show prevalent soil profiles including the approximate depth of each layer. These maps can be very helpful to the trail planner. Your local conservation district or conservation commission may also be helpful. More on the different layers and how they influence the trail planner later.

There are several ways in which soil fails to support hiking use:

Compaction

Hiking traffic compacts the surface soil horizon into cementlike hardness. This compacted surface loses its pore space and its ability to absorb surface water. If this water is not absorbed into the compacted soil, it will puddle on the trail creating an ever-widening mudhole as hikers walk around its edges to avoid it; or, if on a slope, water will start to flow downhill and cause surface erosion. These tendencies make good trail drainage critical to long-term viability and soil retention, even on flat trails.

Surface Erosion

Layout, soils, use, and drainage are the most important factors affecting erosion. Erosion is a natural process in which soils are worn away by wind, water, glaciers, and other natural elements. On trails this natural process is aggravated by soil compaction and the churning agitation of hiking traffic. Water flowing over the com-

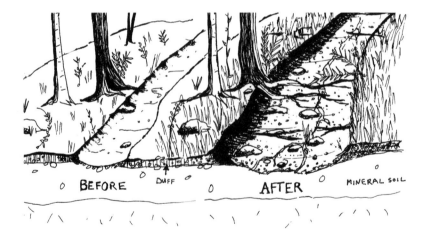

Erosion can turn a treadway into an obstacle course,
complete with exposed rocks and roots.

pacted soil surface detaches the smaller, lighter soil particles and carries them downhill. The greater the velocity of flowing water, the greater the mass of soil carried. Velocity increases as slope steepens; increased water volume also increases velocity. Higher elevations receive more precipitation than neighboring valleys and tend to have thinner soils, particularly in areas with steep slopes and histories of intense logging or forest fires. These large volumes of water, exacerbated by steep slopes and foot traffic, create the most significant erosion hazard on trails in mountain areas. This erosion can quickly destroy a trail treadway.

A treadway in the early stages of erosion is easy to spot. Loose stones and gravel are left after the smaller, stabilizing sand and silt particles have been removed by water. These stones make for poor footing, which in turn causes the hiker to walk on the edge of the trail, thereby killing plants, compacting the soil, and generally initiating a vicious circle of plant mortality, compaction, and erosion that can eventually change a trail into a boulder-strewn gully.

Erosion can cause resource damage beyond the trail's treadway. After sediment-loaded water slows down, soil particles are deposited on the forest floor, suffocating smaller plant life. If these sediments find their way into streams and ponds they can kill fish, degrade water quality, and add nutrients that eliminate the dissolved oxygen plants and fish rely on, a process called *eutrophication*. Soil loss around the base of trees can expose roots to disease and weaken their anchoring function, allowing trees to blow down much more easily.

Because of the possibilities for resource degradation, trail layout, construction, and maintenance in mountainous backcountry must employ a careful evaluation of soil characteristics in order to be successful. Wherever possible, locate trails on soils that are capable of withstanding the amount of use anticipated without eroding or becoming wet and muddy.

The Best Soils for Trails

The ability of soil to withstand traffic of a given intensity depends on several factors. In some cases a single factor can be so limiting that soil will degrade swiftly despite other more enduring qualities it may possess. In other cases a combination of factors are important to consider in determining the best location for the trail. These factors are soil wetness, texture, structure, and depth.

Soil Wetness

Soil wetness is most often caused by poor drainage. Ground water, the height of which is called the water table, moves through the landscape and saturates the surface of soils, especially during periods of heavy rainfall and the spring thaw. The water table fluctuates with the wetness of the season. The seasonally high water table is the highest level of ground water during the wettest month of the year. This seasonally high water table in shallow or poorly drained soils will create problems on a compacted treadway. In very poorly drained soils, such as in bogs or depressions near lakes and streams, water moves so slowly that the soil surface may be wet for much of the year. Avoid building trails in these areas. If you must pass through them, use bog bridges (see chapter 7).

There are several indicators you can use to evaluate soil wetness in the field. The most obvious and simple evaluation is to visit the site after long periods of rainfall or during the spring snowmelt. If much surface water, is evident in many rivulets, then the site may not be right for a trail. Dig a shallow hole along the proposed trail site; if it fills with water or if water placed in it does not percolate down and out of the hole, then there is either a high water table or drainage is inhibited. In both cases the trail will degrade the environment.

Wetlands are defined by plant life. Unless you are a soil scientist, just do a simple check of the plant life of an area to determine whether or not an area is suitable for a trail. Areas with cattails, alders, swamp maple, and other water-loving plants will be wet. These wet areas and their fragile soils are poorly suited for trail locations unless a bridge or boardwalk is provided to keep hikers out of direct contact with them. Staying away from wetlands will also make obtaining a permit, if required, quicker and simpler. Check with your local conservation commission, USDA Natural Resource Conservation Service office, or Agricultural Extension office for wetlands indicator species plants in your area.

Soil Texture

Soil texture refers to the relative proportions of various-sized groups of grains in a mass of soil. It is an important characteristic in the ability of soils to sustain foot traffic. In general, loam soils with a mixture of sand, clay, and silt will resist compaction and erosion most successfully. The smaller sizes of silt and clay particles add cohesion; sand and gravel lend porosity and water absorption. These moderately sandy soils will resist compaction and will absorb a high level of rainfall, making them good for trail use. Use caution, however, when building trails across pure sand. Sand blows when dry, supports few plants for soil retention, and can lead to a shifting treadway.

Inspect soil texture in the field by feeling with the fingers and using a magnifying glass. Look for the following:

Silt—Loose sedimentary material with rock particles less than 1/20 mm in diameter. The finest class of soil.

Clay—A fine-textured soil which usually breaks into clods or lumps that are hard when dry; quite plastic and sticky when wet. The least water-permeable class of soil.

Sand—Loose, single grains; individual grains readily seen and easily felt. The coarsest type of soil.

Loam—A mixture of different grades of sand, silt, and clay with organic material; it has a gritty feel, yet is fairly smooth and plastic.

Soils made up mostly of silt and clay will be muddy when wet, cracked and dusty when dry. These soils erode easily and if possible should be avoided for trails, especially on steep slopes. Coarse fragments in the treadway can increase the durability of the soil. Gravel-sized fragments embedded in the soil matrix help to hold the more easily eroded sand, silt, and clay particles in place, and they also improve soil drainage. Loose gravel on the trail surface can cause uncertain footing, but is not a serious limitation for a trail. Rocks and stones, while making footing somewhat variable, are not serious limitations to trail placement. In fact, they can be natural erosion retardants when used in a hiking trail treadway.

Soil Depth

Soil depth is the distance from ground level to bedrock. Avoid shallow soils when possible. Shallow soils over bedrock or hardpan (an impervious layer of subsoil) can lead to problems on hiking trails. Because water cannot drain downward, shallow soils are often heavy and saturated with water, causing them to erode quickly and slough off when walked on. This is especially true in steep terrain, where steep rock slabs can become dangerously exposed after some wear from hiking. Hikers seeking safe passage use plant life on the edge of the trail for handholds, killing the plants and aggravating trail widening problems. This process is mostly unsuitable to enjoyable hiking and disruptive to the natural environment.

The limitations of soil depth are especially critical in the alpine zone. The soil mantle here is only several inches thick and plant life is small and easily damaged by foot traffic. In the alpine zone the maintainer must take special pains to mark the trail without any abrupt turns. In this way, shortcuts are discouraged. Lining the path with rock scree—and in extreme cases low rock-scree walls—will help to contain the impact of hiking traffic on thin alpine soils to a small area.

Soil depth and grade are the most important factors in determining the appropriateness of trail location. They are both easy to measure in the field with a soil auger, by eye, or with an inclinometer. Therefore, they can usually be evaluated during the initial phases of a proposed trail installation.

CHART 4.1

SUMMARY OF SOIL INDICATORS FOR EVALUATION OF A PROPOSED TRAIL INSTALLATION

Conditions	Conditions Posing Slight Limitations for Trail Installations	Conditions Posing Moderate Limitations for Trail Installations	Conditions Posing Severe Limitations for Trail Installations
Soil Wetness	Depth to seasonal high water table 4 feet or more; well drained to moderately well drained	Depth to seasonal high water table 1 to 4 feet; excessively drained	Depth to seasonal high water table less than 1 foot poorly drained
Soil Texture	Particle mixture of sand, clay, silt; 20–50% of content gravel	High sand content; less than 50% but greater than 20% of content gravel	High clay content; no gravel
Soil Structure			Hardpans less than one foot from soil surface; peaty, muck soils
Soil Depth to Bedrock	Greater than 3 feet	1.5–3 feet	Less than 1.5 feet
Slope*	0–5%	5–20%	Greater than 20%

*Slope is the number of feet of vertical rise per 100 feet of horizontal distance, expressed as a percentage—that is, a 10% slope rises 10 feet vertically for every100 feet traversed horizontally.

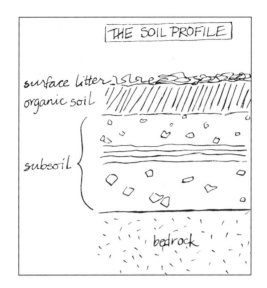

Soil Horizons

As part of soil depth, the various soil horizons are also important, and there are certain horizons that should be avoided. Essentially, the soil profile is made of two major components—the organic layers and the mineral layers. There are layers within the organic and mineral profiles that you'll want to avoid for trail layout; peats, clays, or thick organic layers should be avoided.

While soil was defined earlier in this chapter as "the product of climate and organisms acting, destructively and synthetically through time, on rocks," that definition is not quite the whole story. In fact, the definition of soil and the naming of its parts depends on the function the soil serves. Agronomists view soil differently from engineers, who view it differently from the pedologists, foresters, ecologists, microbiologists, and laundry companies with their favorite "ground-in dirt." The following material is generic information that is intended to help the trail planner find the best soil horizons for the trail. Keep in mind that soil horizons and types can vary in locations just several feet away from each other, and that many of the following layers may be absent:

Organic Horizons

Organics are five times lighter than the more common mineral soils. Trails on these soils are soon on exposed rocks and roots or become excellent examples of saturated muck. Organic soils also have high water-holding capacity on a weight basis: an organic soil can hold two to twenty times its dry weight in moisture, while a mineral soil will hold only about a fifth of its weight in water before runoff.

The organic horizons include O1 and O2 (also known as OL and OF & OH) of mineral soils and mor (fibric soil), moder (hemic soil), and mull (sapric soil) layers of organic soils. In the woods, trail planners will generally want to find thin layers of organics, as the top organic layer is fire-raked down to the more durable mineral layer (if the organic layer is not more than a couple of inches thick). On ledge, any soil should be carefully preserved, as the soil thickness is quite thin.

The first organic layer, or O1 (O for horizon, 1 for first layer; it is sometimes referred to as OL for "leaf layer"), consists of unincorporated matted and or compacted organic material containing large amounts of fiber that are well preserved and readily identifiable by the naked eye as botanical in origin. This material and fiber usually include leaves, forest duff, peat soils, alpine humus, plant litter, and the like. O1, in soil terminology, is fibric soil or mor humus. This layer is always scraped off during trail construction.

O2 is the second organic layer, and occurs where O1 becomes mixed with the mineral component of the parent material by earthworms and other soil organisms or weathering. The original plant material becomes highly decomposed, and its botanical origins are no longer discernible with the naked eye. O2 contains less fiber, has a greater bulk density, and holds less water at saturation than O1. O2 contains what are called sapric soils. This layer can be suitable as a trail surface, provided the treadway is well drained.

The next layer, OF or OE, is found only in some places. It contains intermediate soils with partial decomposition (these soils are called moder, hemic, and folist). The first striking property of these soils is their color, often dark brown or black. The second striking property is that OF or OE soils can be very wet. These soils often form in areas of marshes, bogs, and swamps where conditions are suitable for the accumulation of organic deposits. You may also notice the great view around these soils, as they are common in colder alpine settings, where weak soil-organism populations produce thin soil depth that offers scant frost protection. Soil profiles with this horizon should always be avoided for trail location. Should you have no choice, bog bridges will be required to preserve the soil and protect water quality.

Mineral Horizons

The mineral horizons—layers A, E, B, and C—make the best treadway.

The first mineral soil layer (and first below the organics) is A, where decomposed organic matter accumulates within the mineral soil to form a dark admixture. Often "dirty" from the rich organic contribution, the A layer is what we most frequently walk on. Depending on the particle sizes of the mineral soil and the drainage provided by nature and the trail builders, layer-A horizon soils provide a very durable and predictable footbed.

Next comes the E horizon where clay, iron, and aluminum (the third most common element on earth) oxides wash from the soil and certain resistant minerals, such as quartz, accumulate.

After E comes B, where clays and hydrous oxides commonly reach levels of maximum accumulation. Organic matter collects here more than in E but much less than in A. Blocky and prismatic soil structure is at its maximum here; thicker E and B layers are good for the trail planner, but E and B can be muddy when wet, and dusty and cracked when dry due to the clays in them.

Finally, the fourth mineral layer, C, is found where chemical weathering but no biological weathering takes place. An accumulation of Ca and Mg carbonates resulting in cementation is often found in C; C is also called "hardpan." This level is referred to as the subsoil, while those above are called topsoil. Beneath this horizon is the remaining regolith (R) or just plain bedrock.

Keep in mind that a simple hiking trail can contribute to the actual erosion of tons of soil. Do your best to find the most suitable location in regard to soils for your trail.

Trail Layout

This is the stage where you finally venture into the woods and begin the physical task of building a trail. After going through the visioning and planning stages you'll know which features you want to incorporate, and you'll have secured the support of the public and private parties involved. Apply all of the information in chapters 2, 3, and 4 as you lay out your trail. Above all, always keep in mind the primary objective of providing for the recreational needs of hikers with the least amount of impact on the land. Remember, good layout satisfies the needs of the hiker and is environmentally stable.

Before you start to nail down your route, talk to local people, especially older residents who are familiar with the land. They may be able to point out all the significant features in a particular area and give a broad and personal account of its history.

Aerial photographs can reveal such features as ledges, watercourses, old logging roads potentially usable for the trail, and other detailed information on the land's characteristics. Aerial photos are available from your USDA Natural Resource Conservation Service office or from a managing agency in the case of state or federal land.

Use highly visible flags to mark your route in the woods.

Flagging the Line

Get into the proposed area for your trail and check the route. Then check it again. The more time you spend in the field in this layout phase, the better the trail location will be. Flag the proposed route with engineer's flagging tape. Use a color different from the prevailing color in the area and one bright enough to stand out. Place the flagging at close intervals by tying it securely on living trees and their branches. Avoid putting long tails on your flags—they shred and become litter. Use different colors to flag alternative route possibilities.

Spring and fall are the best times of the year for layout; line of sight is excellent since leaves are off the trees and it's easier to examine tread evaluation when the ground is clear of ice and snow. If there is time, check your trail location at several different times of the year. Check it in the spring for any indication of drainage and wetness problems, and check it in winter if the trail is intended for ski touring.

As you are dropping your flag line in the woods, keep these ideas in mind:

- During layout, pay careful attention to the environmental characteristics outlined earlier in this chapter.

- Where possible always use a sidehill trail location, and check soil characteristics at regular intervals. Keep the gradient below 20% if possible, unless you plan to harden the steep grades during construction.

- Blend your trail into the natural surroundings by maintaining continuity and regularity in the way it traverses land.

- Avoid sudden changes in direction or too much meandering. Likewise, use long, straight sections temperately; they lack interest for hikers.

Practice your orienteering skills. Skilled knowledge of map and compass are requirements for the job. Bring someone else with you. Trail layout is safer, easier, and more fun when done in pairs. One person can scout ahead while the trailing person drops the flag line. Two-way radios provide an extra measure of convenience and safety.

A map and compass will help you plan your route.

Organizing Trail Data

Use U.S. Geological Survey (USGS) topographical maps to record data on the route. If your project is particularly complex, make a card or computer data file that refers back to your map. In this file, record all pertinent features for eventual use in the final on-the-ground layout.

Organize the file in a linear fashion, starting with the beginning of the trail. Describe on each card the nature of a feature and whether it has a positive or negative effect on the trail; also include other pertinent information, such as addresses of landowners if the particular feature is an ownership boundary on private land.

As this information file develops, each feature will become a checkpoint which must either be avoided (a bog or a steep slope) or be included if its effect on the trail is positive (a good view). The final choice of route will then involve connecting positive features and circumnavigating negative ones. As an alternative to a card file, buy a piece of mylar, then overlay natural, cultural, historic, and development features on the mylar. This can also complement a card file.

The layout process is one of trial and error. As it proceeds, you will continually backtrack and reflag the route until finally the location meets the needs of the hiker and lies as lightly as possible on the land. Remember, hikers, like water, seek the path of least resistance. Refine the layout so the trail follows a route hikers are most likely to go.

As you lay out the trail, pay careful attention to where you will install drainage. See chapter 5 and chapter 7 for more information on drainage.

Once your route is flagged and you are satisfied, it wouldn't hurt to get some professional assistance. Find civil engineers, soil scientists, or foresters from your local area by looking in the yellow pages or through your own personal and professional contacts. Ask them to lend their expertise by doing a volunteer assessment of your route.

Vegetation

The type and density of vegetation in areas proposed for trail development have two primary functions in design: aesthetic function, enhancing the hiking experience; and a management function, as a tool to assist the designer in protecting the environment.

Include a variety of vegetation along a trail route to make the trail more interesting and satisfying, especially a nature trail. Likewise, continuity in species composition has its own special attraction: a prolonged stretch of dense woods can promote a hauntingly exciting feeling of anticipation and adventure. Hikers are interested in natural environments. In some cases, though, modified vegetation, resulting from sound timber practices, farming, or other activities, can be interesting and educational, and valuable in providing views and wildlife.

There is no single criterion for making an aesthetic choice between one type of vegetative cover and another. In fact, the aesthetic quality of vegetative cover will usually be a secondary consideration. Place your primary design emphasis on the characteristics of soils and topography—these have a greater influence on trail stability in mountainous and unstable terrain.

There are several ways you can use vegetation in trail design:

Use it to channel and contain hiker traffic. Treadway boundaries are profoundly affected by the density of trailside trees and shrubs; therefore, dense undergrowth enables greater flexibility in trail layout. For instance, switchbacks are less likely to be bypassed by overly enthusiastic hikers if dense shrubbery lines the edge of the trail.

Use it to retard trail erosion. Roots of trailside vegetation anchor soil and retard soil erosion on the treadway. However, with particularly unstable soils, steep slopes, and high visitor use, root stability is not sufficient to prevent resource damage.

Use it to protect from the weather. Experienced hikers know the value of tree protection, especially after having descended from the alpine zone in bad weather conditions. Vegetative cover is most important to the designer in the planning and location of campsites, where protection from the elements is a requisite of good site location.

Use it to buffer and insulate hiking activities. In our crowded parks and forests, vegetation breaks up lines of sight and absorbs sound. A good example of the ability of vegetation to buffer sound is in snowmobile trail design. Proper buffering using vegetation, hillsides, and other features can reduce snowmobile sound levels by one-third to one-half. Vegetation is also a valuable buffer between a trail with high public use and a sensitive environment such as a pond shore.

Use it for building material. Trailside trees are a major source of building material for treadway reconstruction, particularly when rock is not available. The availability of trees of suitable size for treadway hardening may be a factor in whether or not a trail is routed through fragile terrain such as a bog or marsh. Use native trees for hardening to keep costs low and add to the natural character of a trail. More on this in chapter 6.

Use it to indicate soil characteristics. An informal examination of vegetation can indicate broad soil characteristics. Tree size and age indicate soil fertility—large, young trees indicate deep, well-drained soils while small, stunted trees and wetlands species indicate marginal soil conditions.

The preponderance of a species can give clues to soil texture, depth, and wetness. Pine and oak are characteristic of sandy soils, while fir, spruce, and hemlock indicate shallow soil depths. Swamp maple, cedar, and tamarack grow in soils that are moist and boggy for much of the year. Ground cover and understory composition are also indicative of soil characteristics. Check with your local conservation commission, USDA Soil Conservation Service office, or Agricultural Extension for specific indicator plants in your area.

Construction

After you've laid out the trail you are ready to build. Before you start digging, be certain that you have the required permits or other regulatory approval you may need.

Construction is an ongoing process that changes from trail building to maintenance. Once the trail is "worn in" by use, you'll find there are places that need more drainage, some stone steps, or maybe even a short reroute.

The initial construction itself is really quite simple. It has three parts: brush and blowdown clearing, duffing, and marking.

Brush and blowdown clearing and marking are nearly identical in the construction phase as in the maintenance phase, except that you're starting from scratch. Refer to chapter 5 for instructions and information on brush clearing and marking. Avoid cutting out large trees.

Duffing

Begin duffing once the brushing is completed. Duffing is the preparation of the trail tread for foot traffic, and involves scraping away any organic materials (the O1 layer or duff) like leaves, needles, roots, and bark; decomposing vegetation; and any organic soil (O2 or decomposed organic materials). Scraping down to mineral soil keeps the tread drier, defines the trail, and will help it wear in more quickly.

Without duffing and with a little bit of use, a trail with lots of organic material becomes a wet and slimy tangle of mud and small roots.

To duff, use a hazel hoe, mattock, or a fire rake. To ensure a uniform tread, mark each side of the treadway to your tread width standard with string or sticks before you begin. Dig down to the mineral soil, and scatter organics off the trail. Pull the duff onto the downhill side of the trail. Chop out the dense mat of fine roots that forms beneath the duff with a fire rake. Use a root ax for the bigger roots, but only when they present a trip hazard.

When building new trail along a sidehill, cut and fill (also called sidehilling) to create an even tread with a slight downward slope of about 2%–3% to allow sheet drainage to cross your trail at a perpendicular angle to the direction of foot traffic. Flatten any berm on the downhill side to allow water to flow across and off the trail.

Final preparation of the treadway will depend upon your standards for the trail and who will use it. If the trail is near a road and used by lots of families and small children, consider a higher-standard, smoother trail with many of the roots and rocks removed. Leave the roots and rocks on a little-used trail deep in the backcountry.

After your trail is built, your goal remains the same—to provide a trail that satisfies the recreational needs of hikers and lies lightly on the land. To continuously achieve that goal, your trail will need regular maintenance.

CHAPTER FIVE
Trail Maintenance

Just like a car, garden, or house, trails require regular maintenance, or little things will begin to go wrong and lead to bigger problems. Just as a failure to clean the gutters on your house could lead to expensive water damage during a big storm, failure to maintain the drainages on your trail can lead to damaging erosion. In both cases, your initial investment (money and hours of labor) has been wasted. Constructing drainage takes a lot of time—rocks have to be located, excavated, moved, and installed; trees have to be felled, limbed, peeled, bucked, moved, and buried; and there is always lots of digging involved. Cleaning drainage helps to ensure a good return on a trail crew's initial investment in building a trail.

Basic maintenance keeps a trail usable. Without it a trail will revert to its natural state, or worse, damage the resources around it. Basic maintenance involves four tasks, listed below in order of priority. All should be done at least annually or as needed:

- cleaning drainage
- clearing blowdowns
- brushing
- blazing or marking

Many people still believe clearing blowdowns and painting blazes are the most important maintenance tasks. In the East, with substantial annual precipitation and heavy use, the most important word in trail maintenance is drainage.

Cleaning Drainage

Clean drainages to prevent large-scale soil erosion and the costly reconstruction that must follow. Soil is the one thing that cannot be replaced on a trail. Clearing blowdowns, brushing, and marking do protect resources, but they largely ease hiker passage and keep a physical trail corridor open. Cleaning drainage falls into a different category—it is the work of a conservationist. The other chores—marking, cutting brush, clearing blowdown—will not seriously damage a trail if not done. The trail may be more difficult to find or follow, but the treadway will not deteriorate if a trail is not brushed. A maintainer can always go back and blaze, or cut brush. But if a maintainer does not clean a trail's drainage, the results could be cumulatively disastrous for the trail.

If you are not familiar with the various aspects of drainage, see chapter 7, which examines drainage and its construction in far greater detail. This section describes only the cleaning of drainage.

The physics involved in drainages is simple. Trails are a perfect place for water to continue its endless journey downhill. Water seeks the path of least resistance, and it finds much less resistance moving

---

THE RIGHT TOOLS: DRAINAGE

The tools needed to clean a drainage depend on the type of soil and the extent of debris in the drainage:

▶ Use a pick mattock with rocky soil and drainages that are heavily clogged. A grub hoe also works.

▶ For fully clogged drainages, use a pair of loppers to cut small, tough roots that have grown in.

▶ For more neglected drainages, use a root ax.

▶ Use shovels or fire rakes for final shaping, or for touching up drainages that just need light cleaning.

A clogged drainage, like this one, will not drain the trail properly and makes it more susceptible to serious erosion.

down a trail than it does moving down the same slope in the woods. There is less duff, fewer roots and rocks to impede its journey, and once it gets on a trail, water is going to stay there unless the terrain or a drainage moves it off.

Moving down a trail, water gathers speed. As it picks up speed, more water joins in from the side of the trail. Soon a destructive torrent is formed that washes soil away as it eats into the trail. Erosion can be just as devastating to a trail over many years as it can be during a flash flood. Exemplary trail maintenance involves the continual cleaning, maintenance, and protection of all drainages on a trail.

Drainages that have not been cleaned regularly will often be difficult to find. Drainages filled with topsoil, rocks, and leaf litter can be obscured from sight; but you can recover these lost drainages, particularly if they are water bars made of rock or earthen drainage dips. Log water bars buried for long periods of time may be rotten and in need of replacement. Search for lost drainages on a trail by looking for random pin rocks, outflow ditches off the trail, or even the tops of rocks or logs protruding from the trail in a telltale diagonal line.

Once a drainage has been located, clean it and restore it to optimal working condition. Don't just kick the leaves or dirt out of the drainage (something often recommended to hikers by land managers). Kicking is better than nothing, but just barely. Drainages must receive proper maintenance to be consistently effective.

An effective drainage is a wide, flat-bottomed ditch, twelve to eighteen inches wide at the bottom of the ditch and six to eight inches deep. Adequate width is critical, for a small twig and a couple of leaves will clog a narrow ditch very quickly. The ditch's sides should slope gently out and up; vertical walls crumble or slough off into the drainage and decrease overall width and contribute to clogging.

Begin cleaning at the high end (usually the trail end) of the ditch and work down. Scatter all organic matter pulled from the ditch (leaves, roots, and highly organic soil) well off-trail and downslope, where it won't wash back into the drainage. Use mineral soil pulled from the ditch to backfill on the downhill trail section of a water bar or drainage dip. Continue to move down the ditch, clipping and removing any roots and digging out all rocks. Smooth and pack the sides and bottom of the ditch, and pack excess mineral soil onto the backfill with a shovel or your feet.

Don't pack up and move on to the next drainage when you've finished the ditch section on the trail—you still must clean the outflow section of the ditch. A drainage will not be fully effective unless the outflow ditch is wide and clear. The outflow ditch permanently removes water from the trail and assures it won't find its way back on. This section of the drainage is critical, and is often much longer than the trail-end section of the ditch. Length will vary depending upon trail alignment; a trail moving straight down a very gradual or almost imperceptible slope requires an outflow ditch of fifteen feet or more to assure removal of the water, while a trail that follows a contour on a steep hill needs only a three- or four-foot outflow.

Widen the outflow ditch gradually as it moves away from the trail, so it ends in a flat flare allowing water to disperse and saturate the ground rather than creating an erosive, consolidated stream. The outflow will often be the most clogged section of a drainage and will likely require more work.

Once you've met the standards described above, move on to the next drainage with confidence, knowing that the one you just finished will be working hard to protect the treadway and the trail for some time to come.

Clearing Blowdowns

One of the first tasks of spring is patrolling trails to clear trees that have blown down onto or hang over the trails. Clearing blowdown eases passage for the hiker. It also protects resources because hikers tend to create bootleg trails around uncleared blowdowns.

Clearing blowdown opens trails for early season hiking use, reduces complaints, and offers an opportunity to assess the upcoming season's work needs. AMC crews complete a "patroller's report" (see chapter 11) after each trip, detailing the conditions they find on each trail. Covering trails early in the year also gets maintainers in shape for strenuous work in the fast-approaching maintenance season. Patrollers should carry, in addition to their axes, bow saws, crosscuts, or chain saws, an adze hoe or small mattock to clean water bars and other drainages during their travels. For clearing blowdown, the AMC's staff trail crew prefers the ax for its light weight, ready availability, low cost, and ease of maintenance. Because its blade cannot get pinched as a saw's can, many maintainers

---

THE RIGHT TOOLS: BLOWDOWNS

► chain saw, crosscut saw, ax, and/or bow saw

---

find an ax easier to use. With proper training and practice, an ax can be very effective and quite safe.

Patrollers should work in pairs, leapfrogging from blowdown to blowdown. This technique allows patrollers to cover significant distances in a day—anywhere from five to ten miles, depending on the number of blowdowns encountered, the number of drainages to be cleaned, and the terrain. Pairing up also provides a measure of safety in case of accidents or other problems. Remember, stay far away from your partner's saw and flying ax!

In the most common situation a blowdown lies across the axis of a trail within six feet of the ground. This type of blowdown usually requires two cuts, one on each edge of the trail. Remove the centerpiece and discard it off the trail. Some smaller blowdowns require only one cut and then the top can be thrown off the trail. Move all debris at least ten feet off the trail, and make sure all drainages are cleared of blowdown debris.

Trees sometimes fall entirely into the trail or their tops break off and hang down onto the trail. Removing these blowdowns is

time-consuming—the tree has to be cut into manageable pieces that are rolled or carried off the trail. Again, move debris well off the trail, and completely clear all drainages of blowdown debris.

Exercise extreme care with leaning or hanging trees; limbs or tops can snap off and become "widow makers," even if you aren't married. If a tree is not impeding passage, leave it. Even if it is a leaner or hanger impeding passage, consider very carefully the danger involved in cutting it, and consider leaving it as an option—mother nature will likely bring it down safely in the next windstorm. Be very careful when cutting trees that are bent under tension, since they may spring back and cause serious injury. The same applies for tree butts with roots still anchored; they may snap back to a vertical position when you cut them.

If a very large blowdown crosses the tread perpendicularly, cut a notch or steps into the tree to allow passage. Some blowdowns are actually helpful. Leave in place blowdowns that might serve as barriers to unwanted vehicle traffic, as long as hikers can negotiate passage over or around them. Remove them if there is no clear passage for hikers.

Brushing

A well-brushed trail is one on which a large hiker with a big pack can walk without touching limbs, trees, or brush. Footing is clear and the trail is easy to follow because the line of sight, both forward and back, is open and unobstructed. Branches of trailside shrubs,

THE RIGHT TOOLS: BRUSHING	
▶ loppers	▶ hand pruners
▶ bow saw	▶ pole saw (for ski trails)

weighted down in wet weather or with snow, should not obscure the trail, and they should not soak passing hikers.

Brushing means clearing the brush from established trails. Without a regular brushing, even frequently used trails can dissolve in just four or five years into a nether world of undergrowth. In addition to clearing brush you should also put nearby brush in standard condition, maintaining adequate clearance in width and height for comfortable hiking.

The Door Technique

To brush a trail, we recommend the door technique: while strolling down the trail with clippers in hand, imagine you are carrying a door, like a shield. The door is as high and wide as the desired right of way or standard for the trail. The door determines what gets removed and what doesn't.

Width

The proper width for a cleared trail varies with terrain and vegetation. A four-to-six-foot clearance suffices in most situations. In thick growth or in very remote areas a three-foot clearance may be most practical and possibly even desirable, if it adds to a feeling of remoteness.

In high-use areas and on steep slopes with thin, unstable soils, a narrow trail may be desirable because the nearby roots of trailside trees, shrubs, and grasses stabilize soils. A narrow trail is not a panacea; unstable soils on sloping trails under heavy user pressure will deteriorate regardless of how narrow the trails are. A narrow treadway can contain trampling, though, and therefore reduce hiker impact.

Height

Normally a trail is cleared to a height of eight feet, or as high as one can reach. On slopes, stand uphill from your work to reach high

Brushing a trail's right of way to an appropriate width.

branches easily. Where trees are large enough, leave a canopy over the trail to dampen the growth of shrubs, weeds, and grasses. Of course, if you want *more* trailside vegetation, encourage the growth of wildflowers, grasses, and shrubs by clearing back the canopy to let in sunlight. Be careful: you can easily achieve a scorched-earth effect and make the trail corridor look like an interstate corridor by mistake. Leave alone some of the most attractive trees and shrubs.

If a trail is popular in winter, the maintainer should clear it twelve feet high to enable easier travel when snow up to three or four feet deep lies on the ground. Do this high clearing any time of year, but remember that standing on several feet of snow will bring you clos-

Cut branches flush with the tree trunk.

er to your target. Use special tools such as a pole pruner or pole saw for those hard-to-reach branches.

Leave annual growth of grasses and herbaceous plants such as ferns and jewelweed. If annual growth is particularly thick and aggravating, use swizzle sticks to cut it, but be careful of those around you. Don't use machetes and brush hooks on woody growth; they leave pointed stumps and stubs and must be used very carefully to avoid injury. Occasionally pole pruners and pole saws are needed for winter trails requiring high clearing. Where there is heavy growth on a long section of trail, a gasoline-powered brush cutter or clearing saw will save time. Be certain the operator is trained and knows how to use the equipment properly; as always, safety should be the paramount concern. Keep all other workers away from power equipment in use.

Now, back to the door technique. Your imaginary door is as wide and high as your desired right of way. As you walk down the trail, you have the door in front of you acting as a shield. Look for branches, shrubs, and brush that touch the door. Even if it is just the tip of a branch, it should be cut, unless it is a healthy tree more than four inches in diameter that does not impede passage. Low shrubs and young trees should be cut as close to the ground as possible for aesthetic reasons, to prevent tripping, and to keep stumps from sprouting. Avoid leaving potentially dangerous pointed stumps. Remove low growth back to the outside edge of the cleared trail.

Pay special attention to small softwoods and to the lateral branches of larger softwoods. Their needles become wet on a misty mountain day and create a car-wash effect: hikers brushing by them get quickly and surprisingly wet.

Always cut limbs or branches flush with the trunk or stem. Stubs are ugly and can create bothersome and sometimes dangerous snags for packs and clothing. Cut branches growing toward the trail back to the next limb growing away from the trail. Prune trees in this manner to reduce sucker growth, which occurs when a root system geared to provide nutrients to a tree of a certain size causes aggravated growth in the remainder of the tree when a large part is removed. By leaving growth directed away from the trail, you'll reduce future maintenance efforts.

Use the door technique to determine which vegetation should be cut.

If a short treetop has to be removed, then remove the whole tree, since removal of the terminal bud will aggravate lateral growth into the trail and leave an unsightly tree. The same goes for softwoods up to eight feet high. Instead of cutting all lateral branches on the trail side, remove the whole tree, and spare the hiker the sight of an ugly, scraggly tree unlikely to survive.

Trails through alpine areas require special treatment when it comes to brushing. Use judgment and temperance when clearing trails near or above treeline, where the climate is severe and growth rates are very slow. The small trees and shrubs above treeline grow in interdependent communities called *krummholz*. They are like wild bonsai; trees three to four feet tall can be sixty or seventy years old. Removing one tree in a patch of krummholz can jeopardize the other trees in the patch that join roots and branches in protection against wind and cold. Trees below treeline focus much of their growth vertically, but krummholz plants grow out and down to avoid the wind, which is much stronger just three or four feet off the ground.

Tone down the door technique above treeline. Remove only branches if possible when they are growing into the treadway or right of way.

Stay on top of your alpine brushing. If you don't, the krummholz can insidiously spread across the ground, obscure the treadway, and force hikers onto fragile vegetation. The resulting widening of the tread will be difficult to repair, to say nothing of the damage to those fragile plants. Be vigilant, but remember that what you cut will not grow back as quickly as down in the valley.

Cleanup

Your brushing job is not complete until all branches and debris are completely removed from the trail. Pick up all branches, trees, and debris and scatter them off the trail. Avoid piles because they are unsightly and also a fire hazard. In some cases the trail treadway may need to be raked with a lawn rake to ensure complete cleanup and unobstructed footing. To conceal downed trees from hikers, drag them off the trail butt-first until the top is completely off the trail. Large limbs and small trees can be thrown clear of the trail, provided that they do not hang in the branches of shrubs and trees next to the trail or stick up butt-first. Most importantly, remember to clear all drainages of brushing and blowdown debris.

Marking Systems

Trail markings have to work well but should not intrude on the natural experience. The marks must be understandable, systematic, and vandal-proof. The most often used types of marking include paint blazes; plastic or metal markers; signs; and, for treeless areas, posts or cairns. Different trails require different applications of marking. For example, a short trail within a state park that is heavily used by inexperienced hikers might be extensively marked. On the other hand, it may be desirable to have sparse marking on a trail through private land in an urban area or for one in a wilderness area. Sparse

Avoid using a confusing marking system like this one; keep it simple.

Blazes should be well placed, well painted, and obvious to the hiker.

marking of private-land trails helps prevent heavy or undesirable use; light marking in wilderness preserves the wild character of the area and the concept of providing challenge to hikers.

Trail groups are always trying different techniques, particularly when it comes to marking. Some swear by plastic diamonds, others by metal arrows, and yet others by different-quality paints.

Paint Blazes

Paint blazes of oil-based paint are probably the most effective, durable, and commonly used markers on hiking trails (water-based paints such as latex are the easiest to handle and apply, and they also dry quickly, but will not last very long). Paint's durability, universal availability, low cost, and ease of application also make paint blazes the most practical markings on most hiking trails.

The standard blaze on the Appalachian Trail is a white two-by-six-inch mark placed on trees and rocks. For more than half a century, the shape and color of this blaze—the size of a dollar bill (actually two-thirds the width of a dollar bill)—has proven to be visible and effective. Other trails use different-colored blazes of different shapes and sizes. Blazing should be consistent along a trail's entire length; interrupting or changing the frequency of blazes can confuse hikers. Blazes should be neat and well placed. Indiscriminate and indiscernible splotches are confusing and ugly.

As with any paint job, preparation of the surface is at least half of the work. On rock, a wire brush or nylon scrub pad works well to scrape off dirt and lichen. On softwoods with smooth thin bark and on hardwoods with smooth bark, the same tools also work well. On trees with rough bark, such as hemlock or oak, use a paint scraper to scrape a flat, fairly smooth surface the size of the paint blaze. Do not scrape through the bark on any tree, as it will damage the tree and resin will ooze out, discoloring the blaze. Also, do not blaze during rainy or damp weather; paint will run and will probably not adhere to surfaces.

When you paint a blaze, keep the edges neat and don't let the paint drip on the ground or the tree. A one-inch brush works well, and a two-inch brush can be used with a very light touch and will also serve as your template.

After the surface has been prepared, you can apply the paint with ease.

From time to time it becomes necessary to obliterate paint blazes. This may happen when you relocate a section of trail or standardize the marking of a trail section that has been improperly marked. Other changes, such as recent growth that has obstructed the view of a blaze, or the occasional curveball from Mother Nature, may also necessitate the removal or renewal of blazes. When renewing blazes, portions of old blazes that have been widened by tree growth need to be obliterated. To eliminate all or a portion of a blaze, scrape it off the tree with a paint scraper or wire brush, or use a brown, gray, or custom-mixed paint matched to the surface being covered. Use an oil-based enamel paint.

Small quantities of paint in a paper cup are easy to carry, and if spilled will not make a huge mess. Use the wire brush or scrub pad to clean rock surfaces or smooth-barked trees and to smooth spots for blazes on rough-barked trees. The pail is a convenient way to carry all the supplies within easy reach. Some make carrying the pail more comfortable by taping the handle or placing a short piece of old hose over it.

Oil-based enamels, paints, or inks developed especially for boundary marking last the longest and are best to use. The AMC has had good success with a brushable boundary-marking ink from

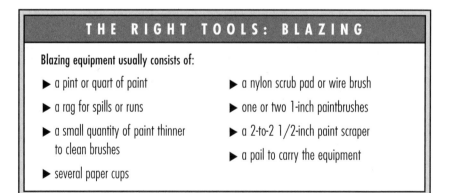

THE RIGHT TOOLS: BLAZING

Blazing equipment usually consists of:

▶ a pint or quart of paint

▶ a rag for spills or runs

▶ a small quantity of paint thinner to clean brushes

▶ several paper cups

▶ a nylon scrub pad or wire brush

▶ one or two 1-inch paintbrushes

▶ a 2-to-2 1/2-inch paint scraper

▶ a pail to carry the equipment

To avoid a mess, carry your blazing equipment in a plastic bucket.

the American Coding & Marking Ink Company. (For other firms manufacturing such paints and inks, see a list of tool suppliers in appendix C.) It is fast drying, easy to apply, and rated to last for five to eight years. Boundaries marked with such paints or inks are often visible for ten to fifteen years or more. Enamels or highway paints are more durable on rock surfaces.

Plastic or Metal Markers

Plastic and metal markers nailed to trees and posts to guide hikers are popular and used effectively to mark many trails. These markers are most effective when a directional marker is needed, or when a marker requires text or a logo to identify or publicize the trail. Plastic and metal markers range from simple, unpainted tin-can tops to custom-designed and -manufactured plastic or aluminum markers. They come in various shapes, colors, and sizes. While these markers are easy to install, they can just as easily be removed by souvenir seekers and other vandals—paint blazes and rock cairns

Plastic and metal markers come in a variety of shapes and sizes.

cannot. Markers can also be expensive, and any color and lettering may fade after several years.

Markers must be carefully installed so they will last. Nails should be made of a soft metal, like aluminum, that will not damage a chain saw should the tree need to be cut. Never use copper nails—copper is toxic to a living tree and will kill it. When installing these markers, drive the nail into the marker and the tree, but leave an inch between the head of the nail and the tree when you are done. Then pull the marker back to the head of the nail. The inch of space between the marker and the tree will allow the tree to grow out along the nail without bending or growing around the marker.

Installing a Marking System

In the installation of a new trail system or in newly marking an old trail, develop a standard system. Color, frequency, placement, and form should be carefully thought out before installation so that changes do not have to be made later. Plot out the color scheme of your marking system on a map of the area, especially if there are a lot of loop trails close together. Blue, red, yellow, white, and orange are good colors to use; they are visible yet not offensive. Think carefully about how your trail will be used, and choose the color accordingly. For example, white is not a good color to use on a ski trail, and red or orange are not good for a trail through a maple grove. Natural colors like brown, gray, and green blend into the surroundings and are not good choices for marking. One may wish to develop a primary color for a main trail in a system and have a secondary color for side trails. This is the procedure used along the Appalachian Trail; the main route is marked in white with side trails in blue. Use care when the trail is located next to boundary lines; boundaries are usually marked with paint, and if the trail blazes are of the same color confusion can result.

Place markers in both forward and rearward directions, perpendicular to the trail, to indicate the route of travel both ways. They should be placed on trees or rocks that are plainly visible along the trail. A large tree is preferable to a small one and a marker on a live tree will likely last longer than one on a dead one. Should the dead tree fall, the marker will be lost. With light-colored markers, darker trees are best for contrast, and vice versa.

Leave a one-inch gap between the marker and the tree for tree growth.

A good way to determine the best place to locate the next marker is to face down the trail ahead as you finish setting each marker or blaze. Quickly note, at a suitable distance, a tree or rock that stands out. Walk toward it, and if it is not too far off the trail, place the next marker on it. On a straight, wide, or well-cleared trail this may be far ahead. Don't limit yourself to marking only one side of the trail. If the trail has a lot of turns or curves, the side with the best visibility or line of sight will vary. Put the marker where those on the trail can see it.

The frequency of markers will be determined by the character of the trail. A good rule of thumb is that a hiker should never have to walk more than a hundred paces without being able to see a marker either ahead or behind. On narrow woods trails with an obvious tread and trail corridor and with little opportunity for the hiker to stray off track, markers can be widely spaced, perhaps every 100–200 feet. On the other hand, a trail without an obvious treadway through an open hardwood forest should be closely marked—possibly every 30–50 feet. This is particularly true if the trail is used in winter. Where trails follow well-worn roads, markers may be spread farther apart. However, if there are many opportunities for one to turn off the road onto other roads or trails, marking should be frequent.

Do not fail to mark the trail because you think no one could possibly get lost in that area. Conditions may be unexpectedly changed by new trail or road construction, lumbering, or blowdowns resulting from storms. Under such circumstances blazes or markers at infrequent intervals may result in difficulty in following the trail. Bear in mind that trail marking is for the benefit of one who is unfamiliar with the trail and terrain. Even if you know it well, many other hikers, some with little hiking experience, will walk that trail. They will rely on your blazes to guide them.

The usual height for marking is 5 1/2 to 6 feet—eye level for many hikers. If a trail is to be used in winter, the markers should be slightly higher. Avoid white as a marking color.

Immediately beyond any crossing road, brook, or trail, there must be a trail marker, even though there may also be a direction sign. Place a second marker nearby, perhaps 20–50 feet from the crossing, in case the first marker disappears.

At important changes in the route, such as turns into a less well defined trail or road, some maintainers and clubs use the double blaze or marker, consisting of two disconnected blazes or markers of the prescribed size, one two inches above the other. This double marker serves as a warning to the hiker: "Stop . . . Look!" The direction of the turn is not indicated with this method. Some trail maintainers will even go so far as to use offset double markers to indicate direction, the top marker being slightly offset in the direction of the turn.

To ensure adequate and proper spacing, treat marking as a separate job for each direction. Blazes should be painted in one direction at a time. Where possible avoid placing blazes on both sides of the same tree since the loss of one tree will result in a twofold loss in marking. It'll take longer, but your marking will last longer and have the same quality and character in each direction.

When a trail is relocated, all blazes or markers on the abandoned section should be obliterated or removed. It is not sufficient to eliminate those at each end, since persons straying onto the old route may see the markers in between, assume they are on the trail, and be greatly misled, possibly with unfortunate results.

Signs

Signs are an essential component of any trail. Signs are usually located at trailheads, junctions, road crossings, and trail features. They indicate the trail name, direction, highlights, facilities, and

distances. Some also have a symbol or abbreviation of the maintaining organization(s). In addition to trail signs, some trails have
special markers made of plastic or metal that refer to a special des-
ignation or point out that the trail is part of a specific trail system.
These markers are usually placed at trailheads or hung at intervals
along the trail.

Wooden Routed Signs—The most common trail signs are made
of wood, with the lettering cut into the sign with a router. Because
the lettering is actually cut into the wood, the sign will be legible
even after the weather has worn off all paint or stain.

Fabrication of Wooden Routed Signs—Unless you use a commercial sign machine, hand-routing wooden signs is a time-consuming process that requires skill and patience. Several types of
commercial sign machines with templates are available, but they are
expensive. However, any artistic person with the proper equipment
can make professional-looking signs using this method. Use the
tricks detailed in this section to make the job easier and faster.

Type of Wood—Take into account workability, durability, and strength, as well as availability and cost. The best woods are clear heart redwood, basswood, Ponderosa pine, yellow pine, white pine, or western fir. In the southeastern United States cyprus and locust are often used. Use good-quality stock, straight and free of knots, checks, and warps.

Size of Signboard—Smoothly planed boards 3/4 inch to 1 1/2 inch thick are appropriate for most routed wooden signs. At trailheads, where large descriptive signs are needed, 1 1/2-to-2-inch stock may be best. The length and width of the sign varies with the length of the message, size of letters, and the sign's importance. Roadside trailhead signs may be as large as two by three feet, whereas directional arrows can be as small as three by eight inches. Because hikers stand directly in front of a trail sign, it is not necessary to make it large, except for the sign at the roadside. Large signs can be made from several boards joined together with dowels and glue, threaded rods, cleats, or similar equipment.

Size of Lettering—Most trail signs will not need lettering larger than 1 1/2 inches in height. Larger lettering can be used for the name of a trail so it will stand out. The text of a sign follows in lettering 1 inch or 3/4 inch in height. The AMC uses 1 1/4-inch letters for the trail name and 1-inch letters for all other text.

SOME DIFFERENT JOINTS FOR 2" SIGN STOCK

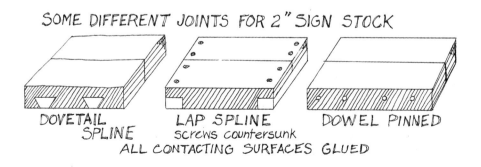

DOVETAIL SPLINE

LAP SPLINE
screws countersunk

DOWEL PINNED

ALL CONTACTING SURFACES GLUED

Stencils—Use stencils to lay out the text of a sign. Letter style should be simple and all capitals. Visit your local stationery or art supply store; many of them sell inexpensive paper or plastic stencils for tracing letters of different sizes. Higher-quality plastic or metal stencils can be obtained from a sign manufacturer, but they may be fairly expensive. Some maintainers, rather than lay out letters again and again, lay out the text on high-quality drafting paper. This can be placed over the signboard with carbon paper in between and the text traced, producing a carbon outline on the signboard. The text can then be filed away for future use. Such reusable texts can also save time when making multiples of one sign or where certain words like "trail" and "path" or lines of text are repeated.

Routing—Before routing text laid out on a sign, practice on scrap wood. Considerable skill is needed to achieve professional results. Use a relaxed, smooth, and steady motion while following the stenciled letters with the router. Practice will make perfect.

Stenciling a trail sign before routing.

A sharp, high-quality bit is essential to good lettering. A dull bit will burn the wood and leave feathers that make painting difficult and have to be sanded out. Use a U-shaped or V-shaped, carbide-tipped veining or grooving bit. Carbide steel, though more expensive than plain steel, is extremely hard and will last much longer and do a better job if used properly. For 1 1/4- to 1-inch letters use a 3/16-inch bit;

Use safety glasses and ear protection when routing.

for 3/4-inch letters, a 1/8-inch bit; and for 2-inch letters, a 1/4-inch bit. Larger letters will require an appropriately larger sized bit. Set the depth of the bit so it cuts slightly deeper than the U- or V-shaped tip of the bit. When routing letters greater than 2 inches, make it easier for the router by first setting the router to cut half the depth of the letter, then go over it again cutting at full depth. Repair mistakes with a little plastic wood filler.

Warning: Using a router bit on plywood may irreparably damage the bit because of the hard glue used to join layers of plywood. When using the router always wear ear protection and safety goggles to protect the eyes from wood shavings or defective bits.

Painting and Staining—Many signs are not painted or stained at all. For instance, signs in federally designated wilderness areas are unpainted to retain a more rustic appearance. Two colors are generally used for painting or staining a sign, one for the background and one for the lettering. Some simply stain the entire sign or treat it with a clear wood preservative. Others stain first and then paint the lettering with enamel. The entire sign can also be painted first with the background in one color and then the lettering painted in another. For contrast, use a light-colored background with dark letters or vice versa. Use a good-quality enamel, not latex, over a compatible primer coat. After the background paint dries, patiently paint the letters. Use a small brush, squeeze bottle, or syringe to nearly fill the routed letters with paint. Then with a small brush, nail, or pointed stick direct the paint so it covers the entire inside surface of the routed letters. Wipe away any mistakes before they dry, and touch up as needed.

Here's a trick to facilitate letter painting: Stencil the sign text on the prepainted board, cover the face of the sign with contact paper, and then route through it. Quickly brush paint into the lettering and pull off the contact paper. Generally, some touch up is needed, and the contact paper and paint do tend to dull the router bit more quickly.

Hanging the Sign—Since you can't stand around in the woods and protect your signs from vandals, hang them securely. One simple and secure way is to hang a sign on a tree or post with two lag bolts. This works particularly well for signs thicker than 1 inch, as the bolts tend to crack thinner signs. Another vandal-resistant (but more expensive) technique the AMC has used successfully is to mount 3/4-inch-thick signs on a backboard of the same size cut from 1 1/2-inch stock. First, lag-bolt the backboard to a tree or post through at least two predrilled and countersunk holes. Then bolt the sign to the backboard through holes drilled through both boards. Fasten small signs to the backboard with two bolts. Bolts should be offset in opposite corners so as not to split the sign along the grain. Larger signs need four bolts. Using sign backing provides a more secure mounting and also helps protect the sign from splitting

Use 3/8" lag bolts to secure a sign to a post.

due to tree growth. All bolts, washers, and nails should be galvanized or at least zinc plated. Standard ones will rust, leaving an unsightly stain on the sign.

Maintainers use many different techniques to prevent theft. Signs that are often stolen can be mounted using special nuts and bolts, such as Vandlgard or Tufnut brands, or you can countersink bolts and cover the tops with wooden plugs or wood putty. If you can, place the sign high out of reach.

The most attractive and effective method of hanging signs is to use a signpost. Trees are not always available or in the right location in the field. Also, posts do not damage trees. A 6-to-10-inch diameter post, buried to a depth of three feet, is best. To make a natural post, use a rot-resistant tree such as cedar, locust, or hemlock, since they will last the longest. Peel the bark off to discourage insects and prevent moisture retention. If you can't get a natural post, use a squared pressure-treated post from a lumberyard.

Bolt the sign to a flattened surface of the post. Bevel the upper end of the post with an ax or saw to shed rain. To prevent turning or removal of the post, place one or a cross of two threaded rods, pieces of rebar, or a large spike into or through the bottom of the post before it is buried; or nail one or two pieces of wood onto the bottom of the post. Above treeline or on ledge, use the pieces of rebar or wood to anchor posts inside stone cairns.

Master Sign List—Develop a master sign list for your trail system. This list documents each sign's location, the text, its condition and when it was last checked. The list facilitates maintenance, repair, and replacement. All AMC signs are numbered and keyed to the master list. The number is routed into the back of the sign or backboard for easy viewing.

Temporary Signs—If permanent signs are not ready when a trail is to be opened or if an important sign is stolen, you need a temporary sign. While they are no substitute for the real thing, decent temporary signs can be made by writing on heavy posterboard with permanent, weatherproof ink, such as that from a Magic Marker. Encase the temporary sign in contact paper to weatherproof it, staple and glue it to plywood, and hang it on a tree or post. A painted piece of plywood written on with a marker will also work. Such signs should easily last one to two years. Check it for fading and animal damage if it must serve longer. Use a dark-colored ink; red and light colors tend to fade quickly.

Other Signs—Some maintainers make signs simply by using a stencil and painting outlined letters on a board. This is a very tedious and time-consuming task, however, and should the paint or painted letters come off, the text will be illegible. We have seen a few signs that were made from plate steel, with letters made with a bead of brazing or stenciled and cut out with a torch. Both techniques are costly, and such signs are generally not aesthetically pleasing in a backwoods setting. For vandal-prone areas they may be

A temporary sign is better than nothing.

desirable, however. Some also use wooden or concrete post signs where the text is vertically routed or cast into the post itself. Since these can be securely buried and tend to be very long and heavy, theft is less of a problem.

Cairns and Posts

In treeless areas, trails are marked with the conspicuous rock piles known as cairns. In the absence of rock, you can use posts. Cairns make attractive and natural trail markers. They are effective year-round because of their visibility even under snow and ice conditions. Well-placed and well-built cairns also help protect the fragile soils of alpine areas by keeping people on a single trail. Cairns are especially important when the weary traveler must find the way in the poor visibility of an alpine storm.

Cairns should be placed along trails that have been laid out in a fairly direct fashion. People will shortcut sharp turns; therefore, it is best to keep the trail curving with the land in gentle undulations. Such trails take the easiest route and represent the most likely choice of travel for the average hiker.

For maximum visibility in marginal conditions, place cairns between fifty and a hundred feet apart at conspicuous locations: a knoll is obviously a better location than a hollow. If a ledge or

The ax shows the relative size of the cairn.

mound is available, then the cairn has greater visibility if placed on it. Occasionally light-colored rocks can be found and used for the top of the cairn, making it more visible. Some paint the upper rock. Paint blazes are also used in conjunction with cairns to mark the route, especially in areas where rock for cairn building is scarce, or where the blaze's color is needed to identify the trail. While large cairns are sometimes used to mark junctions, they do not resist wind and lightning well and should be avoided because of their obtrusive appearance and frequent need for rebuilding.

Construction of Cairns—Cairns should be built to the height of three to five feet. They should be fairly squat, almost as wide at the base as they are high. Cairns constructed in this manner effectively resist wind, frost action, and tampering by hikers.

Take care to avoid damaging areas with fragile soils and vegetation while you are quarrying rock. Find a rock pile near the site that you can reach without trampling plants (i.e., walk on rocks). Carry the rock to the cairn site, or use a rock basket or a skyline (see chapter 6) to move large quantities of rock. Always begin the base layer of your cairn with large flat rocks. With as much flat rock as possible, build each succeeding layer to slope toward the center of the cairn. If this method is used for each succeeding tier, gravity will stabilize the cairn in the same way a stone arch is strengthened by a keystone. Each stone placed on a cairn needs at least three points of contact to be stable and eliminate wiggle. Do not wedge small stones into cracks between large rocks to stabilize them. These wedges may work loose, resulting in loose rocks in the cairn. A strong cairn has each stone stabilized by its surrounding stones.

If rock is scarce or unavailable, simply build your cairns smaller or use wooden posts and paint blazes.

Basic maintenance is critical to the health of any trail, but there is one last thing to remember: take care of drainages first. Before you build cairns, freshen up the marking, or clear the brush on that last quarter-mile of trail, be sure the drainages are clear, wide, and free. While you can always go back and cut brush, paint blazes, or cut out a blowdown, you can't replace the soil that makes up your treadway.

FIRST LAYER

SECOND;
note, joints of 1ST
layer are bridged
by second stones

A WELL MADE CAIRN; rocks lean
toward center, and joints are
broken.

CHAPTER SIX

Building Materials
for Trail Reconstruction

The reconstruction techniques described in the next chapter require that the trail maintainer find native materials in the vicinity of the trail and move them to the treadway. This laborious process should be undertaken carefully to ensure safety, minimize damage to the trail environment, and maximize the efficiency and quality of reconstruction.

As shown in these photographs (above and on opposite page) of the same place on the Lion Head Trail, rock has replaced wood as the preferred material for construction or reconstruction.

The materials, usually rock, wood, or soil, are either found on the surface or dug or cut from sites near the trail but preferably out of sight from it. This is very important—reconstruction material and its source should blend into the local environment.

Service Trails—In major reconstruction projects it is best to gather building materials in several locations and then transport them to the trail using limited-access routes. In this manner damage to surrounding areas is limited to feeder trails which, after construction, can be closed and covered with debris.

Soil for Fill—Occasionally a soil pit needs to be dug to provide soil for fill work along the trail. Though such pits can be dug near the trail, they should be out of direct view, and after being used they should be filled with debris and hidden. Soil can be transported to the trail in sacks, buckets, or if possible, with a wheelbarrow.

Rock Materials

Rock is one of the most useful, and often most available, materials used in trail reconstruction. It lasts longer and is more aesthetically pleasing than other materials. The use of rock as a building material will blend in more naturally than wood, and rock will also last longer and, in most cases, prove more effective. In some locations suitable rock may be difficult to find, move, and work with, but the additional effort is almost always justified. Rocks of many sizes are used for trail definition and mark-

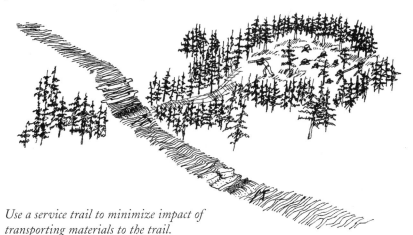

Use a service trail to minimize impact of transporting materials to the trail.

ing, erosion control and drainage, trail hardening, and other purposes.

First determine the amount, size, and shape of rock needed for a project. Then find a quarry of suitable rock. The quarry should be out of sight of the trail and preferably uphill, as gravity and slope will help you move rock to the trail. Usually rock can be found on the surface, but in some cases rock may be partially buried under duff or leaf litter, requiring some excavation.

Moving Rock to Trail

Moving Rocks with Hand Tools

Smaller rocks, like those used for scree or cairns, can be carried to the trail by one person. Remember to lift correctly to protect your back, and watch your step while walking over uneven terrain. Larger rocks needed for steps, rock water bars, and other uses will require additional effort. Sometimes one person alone can maneuver a rock to the trail using a rock bar or muscle power—rolling, flipping, and sliding the rock along. Occasionally several people are required, some working with rock bars and pick mattocks and others pushing with arms or legs.

Where there are boggy areas between rock sources and the trail, crews can sometimes make a skidway by placing dead logs side-by-side over the mud on which to slide the rock across. Rolling rocks through the mud, with its incredible suction power and the slipperiness it creates, can be extremely difficult.

Joint efforts must be carefully coordinated to prevent accidents,

---

THE RIGHT TOOLS: MOVING ROCK

▶ pick mattocks
▶ rock bars

Two trail maintainers double-barring rock.

particularly pinched or crushed fingers. Some people wear work gloves; however, many trail workers find it is better to use bare hands as direct skin-to-rock contact provides a better grip. Also, shifts in the rock can be felt more easily; thus, there is more warning of an impending accident and hands can be pulled clear faster. Though hands may take a beating on rough stones at first, protective calluses soon develop.

Safety

Those working below anyone who is moving rock should have escape routes planned or large trees or boulders picked out to step behind. It is wise for everyone to wear hard hats. Limiting the number of crew working on a particular slope may also be wise; it is possible to have too many people and too much activity in one location.

In some cases it may be best to close a trail to hikers temporarily during construction or at least post someone to direct traffic. Hikers may stand in a particularly hazardous location and

Use a barricade to prevent loss of rocks down a slope.

observe the work in progress, so watch for such bystanders, know where your fellow workers are, and let everyone know when you are attempting a difficult maneuver. Shout a warning if a rock rolls out of control.

Barricades

While working on steep slopes, AMC crews have sometimes built simple log-and-debris barricades next to the trail and below where they are quarrying rock in the woods in order to keep rocks from rolling down the slope. Stack some solid dead logs and a few freshly cut ones to create a backstop into which rocks can be rolled. In some cases barricades are built just on the chance that a rock may be lost in maneuvering it to the trail. Nothing is more frustrating than to spend a lot of time and sweat moving a rock, only to see it slip away and roll off out of sight down the slope. Barricades are also good for the safety of fellow workers and hikers.

Moving Rocks with Winches and Hoisting Equipment

Rigging

A variety of equipment is needed to accompany a winch. Be sure to use rigging that is load rated for the task. To ensure a margin of safety, all rigging should be five times as strong as the loads it is

WINCH AND COME-ALONG BASICS

Winches and come-alongs may prove valuable and even necessary to move rock easily and safely. Moving very heavy or large amounts of rock over long distances may be effectively done only with the help of a winch. Winches are used to control the lowering of rock down a steep slope and are also capable of pulling rock uphill or out of a hole. Large rocks can also be positioned, rotated, and flipped with such equipment.

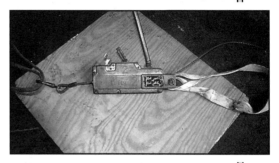

Griphoist shown with anchor and rock sling.

Trail crews have found the grip-hoist manual winch with one- or two-ton capacity superior to the spool-and-ratchet-type winch. The griphoist is a closed-cased device that grabs and pulls, or releases, a wire rope straight through itself. This type of winch has the advantage of ease of operation and the ability to use wire rope of unlimited length. Chain falls, chain winches, and some winches with enclosed casings sometimes do not work well, since dirt and debris get into the mechanisms, jamming them and requiring frequent maintenance. Whichever winch or hoisting device you use, make sure it is rated for the job and be sure to read, understand, and follow safety procedures and operation and maintenance instructions. Use of hard hats and leather gloves is encouraged when working with winches and wire rope, which may develop very sharp splinters.

Never use "cheater" bars on a winch. Safety handles supplied with most winches are generally designed to bend or shear pins will break after a certain load limit is exceeded. Do not overstrain the winch, or its cable or rigging. Snapping cables and rigging can cause serious injury.

Chain-saw-powered "donkey" winches may prove practical for moving rock or logs in some cases. Horses, oxen, or machinery might be feasible, even necessary, to move large volumes of material at times. Generally they are not needed and may not be appropriate for trail work due to the damage they may do to the treadway.

expected to bare; this is also called the *safe working load*. The safe working load of the components will vary depending on how they are set up and used. Inspect rigging regularly for wear and damage; retire any that is questionable. The following is the rigging commonly used by the AMC trail crew:

1. *Nylon Slings:*

   - 3″ Eye and Eye, 4 to 10 feet long, for griphoist anchor and skyline anchors, suspension points, and guy lines.

   - 2″ Endless Loop, 4 to 12 feet long, for choke-hitching rocks to be lifted, extending anchors or guy lines.

2. *Rock basket*—a custom-made nylon webbing basket for wrapping large rock for winching, especially good for rocks expected to roll and tumble as they're moved.

3. *Snatch block*—a pulley, usually with a hook, whose side opens to insert wire rope.

4. *Shackle*—a U-shaped steel piece closed with a heavy pin, used for connecting slings, chain, and wire rope.

5. *Wire-rope clips*—U-shaped bolt with two bolts and a saddle, for connecting or forming a loop in wire rope.

6. *Wire-rope clamp*—A clamp designed to attach to wire rope at any point, useful as an adjustable attachment point.

7. *Rock box*—a 3-foot-square, 6-inch-deep homemade box for carrying scree and rubble along a skyline.

8. *Steel tripods (for treeless areas)*—10-foot-high tripod made of 2-inch-square steel tubing with 1/8-inch-thick walls attached at the tops with threaded rod.

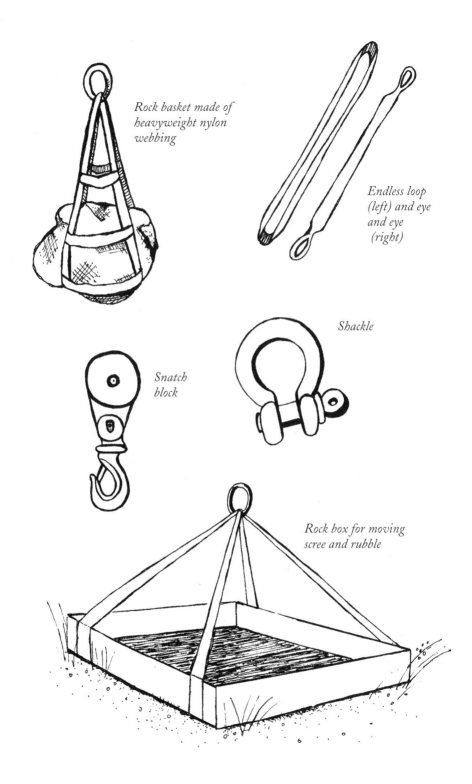

Rock basket made of
heavyweight nylon
webbing

Endless loop
(left) and eye
and eye
(right)

Shackle

Snatch
block

Rock box for moving
scree and rubble

Basic Single-Line Pull

Most of the time winches are used simply to pull, or lower, a rock by dragging it or controlling its descent down to the work site on the trail. Anchor the winch to a large tree by looping a sling around the base of the trunk. A three-inch-wide eye and eye sling around the tree in basket fashion will help avoid chafing the bark and damaging the tree. A large rock or a stout log or rock bar wedged between rocks or trees can also function as an anchor.

Securely wrap and choker the rock to be moved with a two-inch endless loop sling. Encircle the rock a few times, taking advantage of indentations and projections. A rock bar or mattock is often necessary to lift a rock so the sling can be slipped in place under and around it. A rock basket greatly facilitates securing a rock and will hold the rock if it tumbles and rolls.

Always have someone stationed at the winch and at the load. When pulling a rock across the ground, never let the winch alone do the work. Have someone raise the leading edge of the rock with a wedge and unsnag it with a rock bar or mattock when it gets

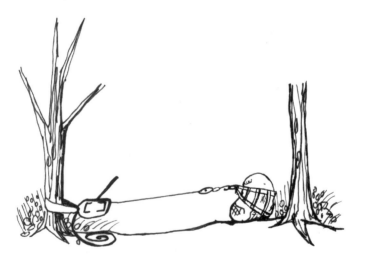

Moving a rock with webbing, winch, and single anchor point.

caught or digs into the ground. On a slope the rock handler should avoid the area below the rock in case it should slip from its hitch.

A 2:1 mechanical advantage can be achieved by hooking a snatch block to the load and running the wire rope through the pulley, and hooking the end to another anchor near the winch's anchor.

The Skyline

The skyline is a somewhat more advanced winch technique. This technique allows rocks to be lifted and transported above the ground from quarry to trail along a tensioned wire rope. A skyline can also be used to transport buckets of soil or gravel and a box or basket of small rocks for scree walls. Rocks can be lowered, traversed across a slope, and even pulled up slight inclines. The wire rope is suspended above the ground by trees or, in treeless areas, by ten-foot-high steel tripods. Transport distances of 200 feet or more can be achieved with a skyline. Although a skyline requires additional equipment and setup time, it has proved with practice to be an efficient, less strenuous way to move large quantities of rock. One of its greatest advantages is that it does not drag rock over the ground; therefore, soils, vegetation, and fragile alpine environments are not damaged.

THE RIGHT TOOLS: SKYLINE SET-UP

▶ griphoist and wire rope

▶ 3 snatch blocks

▶ anchor and suspension slings

▶ slings or basket for wrapping rock

▶ pull rope

Skyline Setup

The first step, assuming there are trees in the area, is to find two appropriately placed large trees (to sling snatch blocks to and suspend wire rope from) and two anchor points. Ideally, the quarry and the project site on the trail should be between and in line with the two trees. The two anchor points, trees or large rocks, should also be in line and far enough beyond the trees so that the wire rope is suspended at a 45-degree (or less) angle from the suspension point in the trees.

Griphoist
anchor sling

Griphois

Place the two suspension snatch blocks high enough in the trees so the rock hanging under the wire rope does not touch the ground. Skillful tree climbing or a ladder will help. Choker the trunk of the tree above a limb or bulge to keep it from slipping down. Do this with a three-inch-wide, three- or four-foot-long eye and eye sling, and hook a snatch block to the free eye. Anchor the griphoist close to the ground so it can be easily operated and hook the end of the wire rope to the anchor on the far end. Put the wire rope in the snatch blocks and feed it into the griphoist, leaving enough slack in the line to reach the load. Put the third, traveling, snatch block on the slack line. Finally, tie a pull rope (one that is long enough to pull, or lower, the load along the skyline) to this snatch block. Now you're ready to sling, lift, and move a load.

Sling a rock so it can be lifted straight up and be held securely while it's suspended. Hook the traveling snatch block to the sling. Keep one person stationed to operate the griphoist and one near the

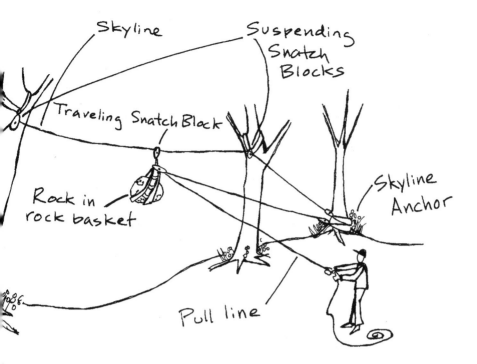

Skyline

Suspending Snatch Blocks

Traveling Snatch Block

Rock in rock basket

Skyline Anchor

Pull line

load to watch and coordinate its progress. The person near the load should be in charge of the whole operation and communicate with the griphoist operator with simple commands such as, "tension," "slack," and "hold."

The griphoist can now increase the tension of wire rope and lift the rock. As the wire rope approaches horizontal its tension will greatly increase. Check all equipment and anchors to ensure they are working properly and holding securely. Once the load is suspended from the taut skyline—high enough to clear the ground during transit—it can be pulled, or lowered, to the work site. To aid in pulling the load, anchor one end of the pull line and run it through a pulley attached to the traveling snatch block to increase the mechanical advantage, or use a second winch. To control lowering, "belay" the load by wrapping the rope around a tree a few times.

Operating the skyline in treeless terrain.

Once the rock is over the work site continue to hold or tie off the pull line. Release the tension of the skyline with the griphoist and lower the rock to the ground. Completely slack the skyline before unhooking the load.

A skyline system is very versatile and adaptable. The setup and operation just described is the most basic and may have limitations due to the terrain, availability of convenient trees, and distance between quarry and trail. To overcome these real-world factors it's a good idea to have extra gear on hand. A selection of slings of various lengths and types, shackles, extra rope, and snatch blocks will allow for greater flexibility of setup and act as spares for failed or damaged equipment. Overall skyline length can be increased by using a longer griphoist wire rope or by having a long auxiliary wire rope for the skyline which is tensioned by the griphoist and its wire rope. Use cable grips or make loops at the ends of the skyline wire rope with wire-rope clips for anchoring and hooking in the griphoist's wire rope.

▶ Always respect the skyline. Even with expert operation it will remain a hazardous system. Hundreds of pounds of tension will routinely be exerted on all the links in the system.

▶ Whenever the skyline is used, place one competent person in charge. This person oversees operation and is responsible for all that happens at the work site.

▶ Designate slings for anchors and slings for wrapping rocks; don't mix them up.

▶ Use only three commands in skyline operation: "tension," "slack," and "hold." The person at the rock calls out a command. The griphoist operator repeats and follows the command until the next command. This will minimize confusion and maximize safety, especially when communication between skyline operators is hindered by weather and/or distance.

Rock suspended from skyline with nylon sling.

▶ When moving rocks downhill always control the descent with a belay.

▶ Stay uphill of rocks and out of the cable's bight.

▶ When using wire-rope clips, "never saddle a dead horse." This means you should always mount the live end of a cable in the saddle of the clamp, not in the U-bolt.

▶ Always have plenty of hardware and slings (both rock and anchor) on hand for setup and operation.

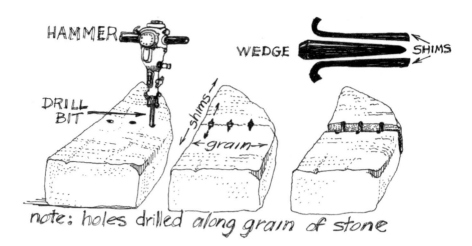

note: holes drilled along grain of stone

Cutting Rock

Sometimes a trail is located far away from appropriate-sized rock. If so, bedrock or large boulders can be split into manageable pieces using a gas-powered jackhammer. Two kinds are commercially available and both are designed to be used in remote locations. The unit, plus gasoline and accessories, can be packed into remote locations to split rock for crews. With training, practice, and a good supply of suitable rock, a two-person team can provide material for a building crew.

Rock, like wood, has grain—an axis plane along which there is a natural weakness. So first, jackhammer a line of holes along the grain where you want it to split. Place shims along the sides of each hole in the rock, then place wedges between the shims. With a small sledgehammer pound the wedges alternately until the rock splits.

When installing split rock put the split side down and out of sight. The drill holes detract from the natural appearance of the trail.

Wood Materials

Cut from trees in the vicinity of the trail, wood is an important reconstruction material. It is used to build stream bridges, bog bridges, and ladders. While wood can also be used for water bars and cribbing, it does not have the durability of rock. When many trees are needed in one location, take trees from a wide area to minimize the impact on the environment.

Find a stand of trees appropriate in size and length located uphill and hidden from the trail. Usually the maintainer has to use what is readily available. If you have the luxury of a choice, spruce and fir are ideal in the Northeast, since they are usually straight, free of large branches, easily cut and peeled, and relatively lightweight. Hardwood, such as locust and oak, can also be good; but in the large dimensions required for good water bars they are more difficult to carry. Conifers such as hemlock, fir, spruce, and cedar are a good deal more rot-resistant than common hardwoods such as beech or birch.

Trees should be felled, limbed, peeled, and cut to appropriate length on-site away from the trail so that bark, wood chips, and other waste products do not litter the trail. A freshly peeled log can be slippery, so some maintainers peel the log at the trail and remove the debris afterward or, if time allows, wait for the log to dry.

Once prepared, logs can be hand carried, dragged, flipped, or slid down to the trail by one or more people. Large and heavy logs can be dragged to the trail or lowered down a steep slope with the aid of a winch.

Size up your tree before you cut your notch.

Felling a Tree

Tree cutting is a skill that can be improved even after years of experience. The inexperienced cutter should learn on small-diameter trees, guided by an experienced feller. With practice the novice can graduate to larger-diameter trees and to more complex cuts that require much preplanning.

Several factors must be considered in order to fell a tree in the direction desired:

The direction and strength of the wind. It is easiest to fell a tree downwind or at right angles to a mild wind. It is hardest to fell a tree into a strong wind.

THE RIGHT TOOLS: TREE FELLING

For ax felling:

▶ hard hat

▶ ax

▶ plastic wedges

▶ sledgehammer

For chain-saw felling

▶ hard hat; ear, eye, and face protection

▶ chaps

▶ gloves

▶ wedges and sledgehammer

▶ felling lever

▶ gas mix and bar oil

▶ chain saw

▶ scrench, files, and gauges

The lean of the tree. It is easiest to fell a tree in the direction it is leaning or at right angles to the lean. With advanced felling techniques a tree can be made to fall in any direction; however, it's easier to bring a tree down in the direction it's already heading.

Large limbs and oddly shaped trees. With big trees, particularly hardwoods, it can be difficult to determine the best felling direction. The cutter has to study the tree carefully to determine how the relative weights of the major limbs, multiple tops, snow and leaf loads, or bends in the trunk will affect the balance of the tree.

Other trees in the area. Great care should be used to ensure that a tree does not get hung up in a neighboring tree as it falls. When choosing the direction for felling, keep in mind that space should ideally be available for the tree to fall to the ground. A hung-up tree can be very troublesome and, when the cutter tries to get it down, potentially very hazardous. The safest way to remove a hung-up tree is to drag the butt back from the direction of the fall.

Safety Procedures

Always follow these safety rules:

- Study the tree carefully to determine if it has what loggers call "widow makers," dead limbs or tops that could break off during the cutting and come crashing down on the cutter. These trees should be avoided. If you do choose to fell it, post a spotter to watch the top and warn the cutter if debris starts to fall from above.

- Clear the area around the base of the tree so that the cutter will not be restricted, confined, or have his concentration disturbed during the cut.

- Clear an exit route away from the direction of the fall, and rehearse exiting several times so the cutter can move quickly out of the danger area. This is also the route the feller will take after the tree starts to fall. If the fall line of the tree is uncertain, prepare more than one escape route. The escape route should be out of the 180-degree fall zone, but not directly behind the desired felling location.

- Before felling, clear everyone well away from the area where the tree could possibly fall. If the tree may fall near a trail, post one or two people on the trail to halt traffic until the tree is safely down.

- Once the tree starts to fall, the cutter should move clear away from the butt of the tree. The danger of "kick-back," the butt jumping back off the stump, is always a potential hazard.

The Ax Cut

The first cut in a tree to be felled is the *front cut*, which is on the side of the trunk in the direction of the planned fall line. Proper preparation of the front cut ensures a predictable fall line. The front cut depth should be about one-half the diameter of the trunk. If no heart rot is evident, a deeper front cut will better guarantee that the tree falls in a predictable manner.

The front cut should be a V-shaped notch of about a 90-degree angle, with no wood chips left at the point of the V. Any wood chips

Trim the puckerbrush and prepare your escape routes before felling.

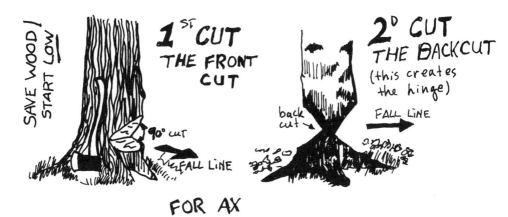

SAVE WOOD / START LOW

1ˢᵀ CUT THE FRONT CUT

90° cut

FALL LINE

2ᴰ CUT THE BACKCUT (this creates the hinge)

back cut

FALL LINE

FOR AX

left will tend to wedge the tree off the planned fall line. The fall line will be exactly at right angles to the back of the front cut, all other factors being equal.

After the front cut comes the *back cut*. Before beginning, check to make sure no fellow workers are in the vicinity of the fall line. Check escape routes one final time before proceeding. Those in the area should be aware of the progress of the cut.

The back cut should be about two-inches higher than, and parallel to, the front cut. As the back cut deepens a "hinge" forms from the remaining wood between the front cut and the back cut. The tree will then fall in the direction of the front cut. As the cutter finishes the back cut he should watch for the first, almost imperceptible movement of the tree. If it is in the desired direction he can proceed.

Minor adjustments in the direction of fall can be made by cutting the side of the hinge opposite the desired direction of fall. For example, for the tree to fall more

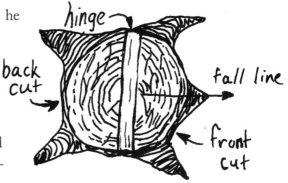

hinge

back cut

fall line

front cut

Top view of a proper ax cut showing hinge.

1ˢᵀ CUT

90° cut

FALL LINE

2ᴰ CUT

beware, don't break the hinge

fall line

FOR CHAIN SAW

to the right, the cutter would deepen the back cut in the left side. This technique can also be used to influence the direction of the fall to counter an undesirable lean.

As soon as the fall begins, the cutter should immediately leave the spot via one of the preplanned escape routes: tree butts frequently jump back or sideways.

The Chain Saw Cut

If a tree gets hung up in another, becoming a "leaner," a few bounces, pushes, or kicks to the butt of the cut will knock it loose. A rock bar, cant hook, or peavey can be used to roll or twist a tree butt to free the top. A winch or rope can also be used. Extreme care should be exercised in any such activity.

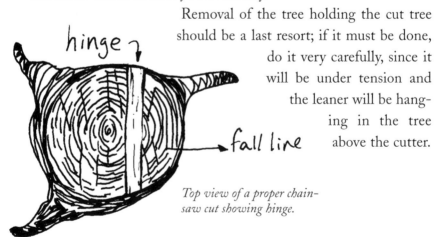

hinge

fall line

Removal of the tree holding the cut tree should be a last resort; if it must be done, do it very carefully, since it will be under tension and the leaner will be hanging in the tree above the cutter.

Top view of a proper chain-saw cut showing hinge.

CHAPTER SEVEN

Erosion Control
and Trail Reconstruction

All land areas have a certain ability to sustain recreational use without damage. Some trails can endure lots of traffic while others, especially in mountain parks and forests with steep slopes, fragile soils, and abundant water runoff, are more sensitive. Erosion-control measures and trail reconstruction increase the land's ability to withstand hiking use without resource damage.

Two factors control the extent of a trail's reconstruction. The first is the volume of use an area receives. More use means more wear and tear on a trail, and therefore more trail maintenance to protect soils and plant life. The second factor governing reconstruction is the character of the land itself. Areas that are wet, are located on steep slopes, have poor soils, or support fragile vegetation such as an alpine zone require particularly careful—and sometimes costly—reconstruction.

When reconstructing a trail, one should minimize the visual impact of trail work and avoid undue infringement on the trail's natural qualities. Overconstruction or excessively regular and obvious construction can degrade the trail environment and hiker's experience.

When to Relocate or Repair a Damaged Trail

Heavily damaged trail sections need to be carefully examined when deciding whether to relocate or reconstruct the old path or relocate the section entirely. Eroded gullies, difficult ledges, or wide muddy areas on trails can be circumnavigated with a relocated section of trail or they can be hardened and stabilized. To decide, ask the following:

- Will the new section of trail have the same kind of terrain as the damaged section?

Often the answer is "yes." If so, it is often best to repair the trail in the old location rather than open up a new trail that will deteriorate in the same fashion. If, however, a bypass can cross the same terrain in a less direct fashion—e.g., if there is a design change whereby the trail will cross the slope rather than climb directly up it—then the relocation is worth considering.

- Will the old section of the trail be too difficult to close and restore?

If the section of trail being replaced is the most obvious route in a given landscape (for example, on a pond shore or on a pronounced ridge), hikers naturally tend to use the trail even after a relocation is built and the damaged section has been closed. In this case, it is best to stick to the old location. Sometimes a relocation can actually hasten environmental degradation when hikers confuse it with the old location and begin using both routes interchangeably. When this happens there can be many problems with both locations; unplanned crossover trails may also develop because of hikers' confusion.

Long relocations should only be used when they result in a substantial improvement in the overall environmental conditions. Short relocations around a wet area or eroded section may be appropriate, but the best long-term solution is usually either to close and relocate a long trail section or to reconstruct it. More often than not reconstruction is the best alternative.

Preventing erosion is the most difficult task in maintaining trails over steep, mountainous terrain, or through wet and fragile areas. Four categories of tools are used to prevent and/or control erosion:

Drainages are probably the most important ally of trail maintainers. Water bars and ditches, for example, can be considered a dynamic form of erosion control. Set across or along the trail, drainages keep or direct water off the trail.

Stabilizers, most commonly steps set to fill the treadway, serve to slow water down and retain soil by reducing the steepness of the slope and creating little terraces. Cribbing is an effective means of holding soil below or above a trail that traverses a slope.

Hardeners are used where a trail crosses wet areas that cannot be effectively drained. Step stones and bog bridges, elevated above the mud, provide the hiker a solid surface. By keeping the hiker out of the mud, trail hardeners not only make hiking more pleasant, but also protect fragile soils and vegetation.

Definers, most often scree walls, channel hikers onto the established treadway or hardened surface, preventing trail widening and protecting adjacent plants and soil from being trampled.

Each erosion-control device fits best in one of the four categories; however, it is important to note that they may also achieve other goals. For example, scree set along the edges of a rock staircase not only defines the trail but will aid in retaining soil along the steps. Bog bridges can also serve as trail definers while performing their principal duty as hardeners.

In most situations a combination of techniques is often the best approach. Along a gullied section of trail, for example, a partnership of rock steps, scree, and water bars assist each other. The water bars protect the steps while the steps hold soil and keep water bars from clogging and their backfill from wearing away. These and other techniques are complementary.

Drainages

Erosion due to running water, made worse by hiker traffic, does the greatest damage to a healthy trail. Water bars are a very effective way to remove runoff from the trail. Water bars may be made of rock or wood but rock is preferable for its permanence and natural appearance.

Rock Water Bars

Use angular rocks with flat surfaces. First dig a deep trench extending beyond each edge of the treadway. Place rocks in the trench either lying flat or on edge with straight, flat surfaces facing uphill toward the ditch. If the rocks are tightly butted end to end or overlapped in shingle fashion, water will not leak between them. Placed solidly and properly, rock water bars will provide a more durable and more aesthetic alternative to log water bars. And of course they are more appropriate above treeline.

Wood Water Bars

Any rot-resistant type of wood, such as spruce, fir, or hemlock, can be used for a water bar. The diameter of a water bar should be at least eight inches at the log's small end. The length depends on the width of the trail, which in some cases can be more than ten feet. It should extend past the outside edge of the treadway on both sides. Peel the bark off the logs so it doesn't come off later and clog the water bar. Peeling may be very difficult with hardwoods or with any tree late in the season. Set the logs so that people and water can't go around either end of the water bar; otherwise, channeling and soil compaction will misdirect water and nullify the water bar's purpose.

Placement

Effective water bars fit the surrounding topography and conditions. On a steep slope where erosion is occurring, water must be removed near the top of the slope before damage can occur. Try to locate where the water enters the trail, and look for a place to remove it quickly. Look for evidence of seeps or springs, leaf litter, soil, and debris deposits showing water movement after spring snowmelt or rainstorms. Check a trail for erosion damage during or just after a rainstorm to see runoff conditions at their worst. When a small stream or some other form of runoff enters a trail, walk up the watercourse to see if it can be channeled away before it reaches the trail. Sometimes jams of debris develop, causing water that was never affecting the trail to flow onto it. Clearing the debris will often return the water to its original channel.

Where numerous small runoffs cross a trail, a ditch may be used to channel the water into one main flow, thus avoiding excessive construction. At stream crossings, where there is a possibility of the flow jumping the channel and going down the trail, water bars might be necessary to stabilize and reinforce the lower stream bank.

Ideally, water should be channeled from the trail without its flow being significantly impeded, thereby preventing it from dropping its load of sediment and clogging the bar. For this reason, natural turns in the trail can be excellent water bar locations because water will more easily be removed and the water bar will be somewhat self-cleaning, an important factor in considering locations. Water bars may tend to misdirect hikers, especially on corners. Log barricades across the outflow ditch will keep hikers on the trail. Be careful that these are placed high enough to avoid plugging up the ditch.

Use a water bar at a corner to drain a trail easily.

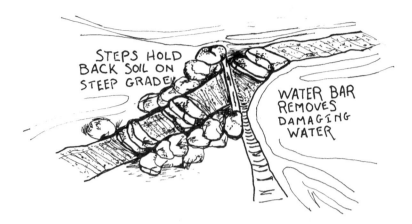

STEPS HOLD BACK SOIL ON STEEP GRADE

WATER BAR REMOVES DAMAGING WATER

The spacing of water bars along a trail depends on the steepness of slope, the amount of runoff, and the availability of places to divert the water. Poorly laid-out or gullied sections of a trail may offer few good placement choices. Excavating larger and longer outflow ditches will ensure that water gets out and stays out of a gully or trail running straight up a slope. On grades of 20 percent or more, every opportunity to remove water should be taken. On lesser slopes water bars can be spaced farther apart.

A combination of steps and water bars is often used on steep slopes, though if soils are quite stable and slopes are shallow then water bars alone may suffice. Creative placement of bars and steps in a complementary sequence prevents the bars from clogging, as loose soil is held in check by steps. Steps in turn are protected by water bars that remove water from the trail and therefore keep the steps from washing out.

In steep-sided gullies where removal of water is difficult, steps may predominate for keeping erosion in check. However, every possible exit for water should have a water bar, even if it requires digging through the walls of the gully.

Installation

Once a site is chosen, the first step is to dig a trench that will hold the water bar. Be sure the trench, and the water bar, extend off both sides of the treadway. Neither water nor people should be able to go around either end of the bar; otherwise, channeling and soil compaction will misdirect water and nullify the water bar's purpose.

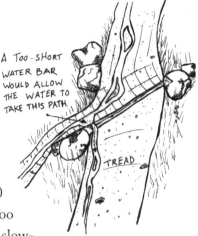

In order to divert the water efficiently, the water bar and its trench must be at an angle, generally 30 to 50 degrees to the axis of the treadway. Too shallow an angle will result in the water slowing down and dropping soil and debris that will eventually clog the water bar. Too sharp an angle, perhaps in excess of 70 degrees, may accelerate runoff, undermining the water bar and increasing erosion damage.

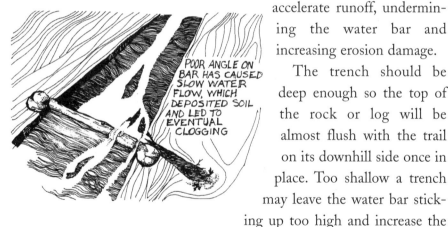

The trench should be deep enough so the top of the rock or log will be almost flush with the trail on its downhill side once in place. Too shallow a trench may leave the water bar sticking up too high and increase the danger of it being undermined. Soil and rock excavated from the trench should be heaped on the trail below the water bar to be used later as backfill. Leaf litter, organic mud, and roots will not make for good backfill and should be disposed of off the trail.

There are two basic ways to construct a rock water bar. The first is called the "cake" method. Use

ROCK WATER BAR
CAKE METHOD

large flat rocks, at least twelve-inches thick, that have a long, straight edge to form the face of the bar. Set rocks flat in a trench the width of the rock, with subsequent rocks set slightly forward of the one below it.

Another way to construct a rock water bar is by using the "toast" method—setting thin, flat rock on edge into a deep and narrow trench. Set rocks so they lean back slightly downhill against the backfill and overlap each other in shingle fashion. This technique works especially well with smaller rocks. Be sure the rocks are solidly set by kicking them in all directions and resetting those that need it.

When constructing a rock water bar, set rocks into the trench one at a time and tightly together, or slightly overlapping each other,

ROCK WATER BAR
toast METHOD

starting at the lower end. Much like shingles on a roof, water will flow from one rock down to the next without going between. No matter which method is used, it's important that all rocks are set securely, as flowing water and foot traffic may dislodge them. Test the stability by kicking and jumping on the rock; ideally there should be no movement. If it's not quite set, try to wedge the rock in tighter or reposition it slightly with a pry bar or mattock. Packing soil around and under the rock may also help. The extra effort it may take to solidly set a rock will ensure that the water bar will work properly and last for decades.

When constructing a wood water bar, place the log in the trench with its larger end at the lower end of the trench. This helps accommodate the greater amounts of water that flow past the lower end of a water bar. The log should fit snugly in the trench with no high point or voids under the log.

A large *pin rock* should be placed on each end of the log to help hold it in place. This is preferable to stakes, often used in the past, because pin rocks are more permanent and will not impede the flow of water or hold debris. Sometimes they are the only choice if soils are rocky or hard, making stake driving impossible. Pin rocks will also serve as barriers to prevent hikers from going around the ends of the bar. Sometimes, with good planning and skillful use of tools, one can wedge the log between existing boulders on the trail.

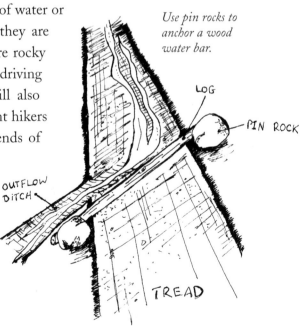

Use pin rocks to anchor a wood water bar.

LOG

PIN ROCK

OUTFLOW DITCH

TREAD

Peeled logs, or unpeeled logs that eventually lose their bark, can be very slippery. You may choose to top the portion of the log across the treadway with an ax, making it rough-surfaced for better footing. Be careful not to remove too much of the log; its reduced height may allow water to wash over it.

Once the bar, either rock or wood, is in place, the next step is to dig the ditch along the uphill side of the bar. Extend the ditch across the entire treadway to capture all runoff flowing down the trail. Starting about four feet uphill from the bar, gradually slope the ditch down to the middle of the rock or log, leaving half the rock or log buried below the bottom of the ditch. A steep-sided ditch will collapse under hiker traffic and clog the ditch. Packing a little soil up against the bottom edge of the bar will help prevent it from being undermined. Soil and small rocks excavated from this ditch should be piled below the bar to be used as backfill.

Backfill the water bar by packing soil up against its downhill side. Using the previously excavated soil and small rocks (do not use any duff, roots, or organic mud), form a well-packed mound behind the bar. The backfill mound should be slightly higher than the bar, gradually sloped, and about two feet wide. With traffic it will compact and wear down to the correct size.

Finally, the *outflow ditch* can be dug off the lower end of the water bar to remove the runoff completely from the trail. The outflow ditch should be broad and flat-bottomed (twelve inches or more at the bottom), free of roots, and obstructing rocks, and with sloped

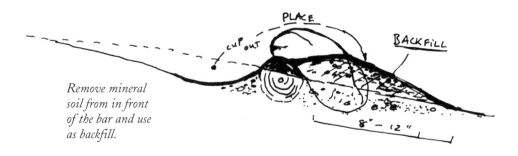

Remove mineral soil from in front of the bar and use as backfill.

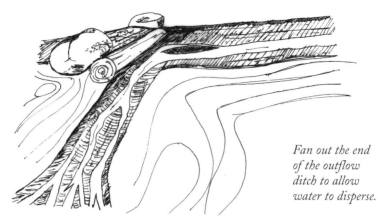

Fan out the end of the outflow ditch to allow water to disperse.

sides. A narrow ditch or one with protruding roots or rocks will clog easily; steep sides are apt to collapse. The length of the outflow ditch depends on the terrain; in any case, it needs to be long enough to ensure that water will leave and not reenter the trail. Fan out the end of the outflow ditch to allow water to disperse and help keep it from clogging.

If water falls or drops steeply off the edge of the trail, line the outflow ditch with rocks to slow the water and protect trailside soils from eroding. This will work much like an object placed at the base of a gutter on a house. In the alpine zone, where plants are small and easily disturbed, this technique is particularly important.

Drainage Dips

Drainage dips, often used on logging roads, are another water-removal technique, and are simple and easy to construct. Dips are

A drainage dip can be used on lesser grades or areas of low runoff where a water bar would be overkill.

DRAINAGE DIP — CROSS SECTION

basically earthen water bars that are useful where the grade is 5 percent or less and runoff is minimal. Only stable materials are effective for the construction of dips; duff and organic mud should not be used.

To make a dip, dig a ditch across the trail at an angle, making a fairly substantial mound (one to two feet high and equally thick) on the downhill side with the soil. Dig at a sharp angle (45–50 degrees) to reduce the force of the flowing water and subsequent erosion of the mound. The mound can quickly break down from the forces of water and hiking traffic. For added strength, lay rocks under the mound as a foundation for the soil. Finally, an outflow ditch similar to one for a water bar should be dug.

Dips may require more maintenance than water bars. In addition to keeping the ditch clear, the mound should be built up periodically with more soil. If a dip doesn't adequately drain a trail, replace it with a water bar.

Bleeders

Bleeders ensure that water drains thoroughly from a trail at a natural low spot or obstruction, like a large rock or root, and doesn't pool up or continue down the trail. Bleeders enhance existing features in the terrain where runoff is likely to be leaving the trail.

To construct a bleeder, dig a shallow depression completely across the treadway, making sure it is pitched toward the low edge of the

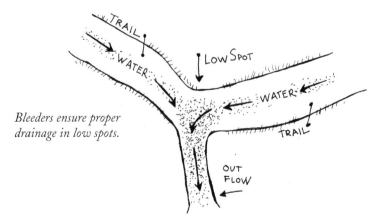

Bleeders ensure proper drainage in low spots.

trail. The sides of the bleeder need to be gently sloped or hiker traffic will wear them down and clog the drainage. Finally, an outflow ditch should be dug off the edge of the trail. A wide, root-free ditch dug long enough to keep water from reentering the trail completes the bleeder and reduces maintenance.

Cross Ditch

A cross ditch ensures that runoff or small streams entering at right angles to a flat section of trail cross completely and flow away from the trail. Dig a ditch large enough to capture and contain all the runoff. Use soil and rocks excavated from the ditch to

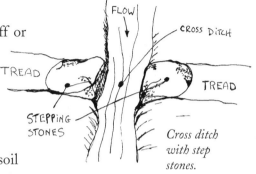

Cross ditch with step stones.

build up the banks on both sides. Where flow is high, line the sides with rock as you would in the construction of a rock water bar. To prevent the ditch's banks from being beaten down by hiker traffic, set a large step stone into the banks on both sides. Finally, dig an outflow ditch.

Drainage Ditch

A drainage ditch along the side of the trail collects water in areas where heavy seepage, springs, or runoff enters a trail and can't be

DRAINAGE DITCH and BAR

immediately removed. When a trail is ditched along its uphill side, water traveling laterally through the soil will be caught in the ditch before it hits the tread of the trail. Then, after traversing the length of the ditch, it can be carried off by an outflow ditch or water bar.

When evaluating a trail section's drainage, use a ditch wherever necessary to develop permanent drainage patterns that will leave the trail treadway elevated and dry. On steep slopes any collection ditches should be drained by frequent water bars to avoid excessive buildups of water that may exacerbate erosion. Extremely large and unsightly ditches should be avoided for aesthetic reasons.

Switchback Drainage

One method of draining a switchback is to direct water on the upper leg of the switchback to its upper side. Then the water, with the use of a ditch, can be properly and completely drained at the apex of the switchback, as illustrated below.

In some cases it may be necessary to drain water off the low side of the upper switchback. If this situation occurs, a second water bar on the lower leg of the switchback may be necessary to remove water completely, as shown in the second drawing.

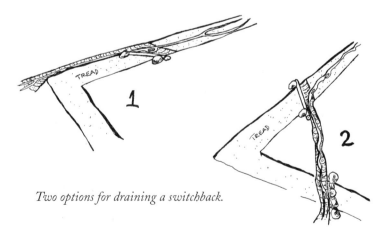

Two options for draining a switchback.

Drainage Maintenance

Drainages should be cleaned out annually in order to keep them working well. Dig out debris; sediments should be spread over the trail below the drainage or added to the backfill. Clean all outflow ditches at the same time, using the debris for backfill. An adze hoe or hazel hoe works well. Sometimes soils can be too compacted or rocky to be easily dug out with a shovel; use a pick mattock. Over time, roots and brush can encroach on the ditch and should be cut back with clippers as needed.

Stabilizers

Steps

Steps provide protection from erosion on steep trail grades. The basic purpose of steps is to provide a stable vertical rise on the trail, which slows water and retains soil. Since they aren't part of the natural landscape, steps should be used only where necessary. Though probably less important in reconstruction than drainages, steps grow in importance as trail slopes steepen and when damage, due to erosion, has already occurred. If a trail has moderate grades, steps can be confined to occasional steep rises and areas just above water bars, where the steps will prevent clogging. However, on steep ascents they may be used extensively and are critical to soil retention and stabilization.

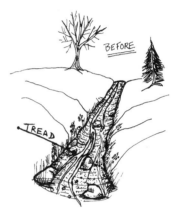

Use rock steps and scree to stabilize a gullied trail.

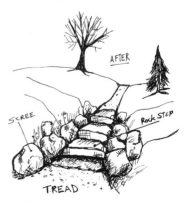

Place steps thoughtfully on the trail to ensure that hikers will use them. They have to be in the most attractive place to walk and must not be too high; otherwise, hikers will bypass them and soon create a new eroded route that others will use. As a general rule, keep the rise to twelve inches or less.

Some hikers avoid even well-placed steps, particularly if they are tired and going uphill. In order to prevent this, install scree alongside the steps. In addition to scree, brush, logs, and other debris can be used. Trails that are located in wide gullies can be narrowed by placing scree on both sides, leaving the steps in the middle. This will serve to both confine traffic to the steps and hold the soil in the banks of the gully.

Rock Steps

Rock steps are far more desirable than log steps, since they last longer and are much more aesthetically pleasing. Over time they will begin to look like a natural part of the trail, especially if they are placed carefully. Even where suitable rock isn't readily available, rock steps are so far superior to wooden steps that the additional effort to obtain them is worthwhile. Any shape of rock can be used; however, a large, flat-surfaced rock is much easier to work with and makes a more usable tread. Rocks should weigh at least 100 to 200 pounds. Smaller rocks are more apt to work loose. The weight alone will help keep a large rock in place.

To place steps, work up from the bottom of a slope. Create a foundation that helps determine the best location for each subsequent

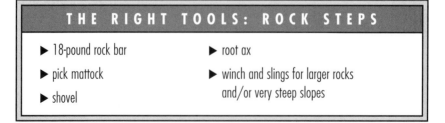

THE RIGHT TOOLS: ROCK STEPS

- ▶ 18-pound rock bar
- ▶ pick mattock
- ▶ shovel
- ▶ root ax
- ▶ winch and slings for larger rocks and/or very steep slopes

step. The first bottom step should be large and set deep, with little or no elevation gain above the treadway. Over time hiker traffic will wear away and compact the soil below the bottom step. If not set deep enough this step could be undermined and jeopardize the stability of the steps above it. On very steep slopes, you may have to overlap steps, resting one on top of another (for these cases you have to work from the bottom up).

Installing Rock Steps

Find a rock with a good, flat stepping surface wide enough to fill the treadway. Maneuver the rock to the trail near the site where it will be placed. Then take a good look at it. Use the side that has the flattest surface as your tread. Dig a cone-shaped hole that will fit the bottom of the rock. The hole needs to be deep and just wide enough for the top of the rock to be at the desired height. The rock should fit in the hole so its perimeter rests on the sloping sides of the hole and not on the bottom, or it will rock back and forth. It should sit like a scoop of ice cream in a cone. Three solid and widely spaced points of contact are ideal and will keep the step from rocking.

Once the hole is dug, maneuver the rock so it can be lowered, flipped, or slid into the hole. Try to get it right the first time: once a large rock is dropped into place it may be very difficult to pull it back out and reset it, especially if the trail is muddy. Use pry bars

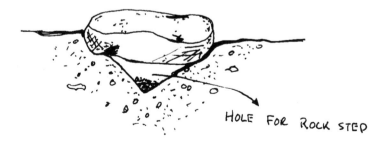

Use a cone-shaped hole to securely set a rock step.

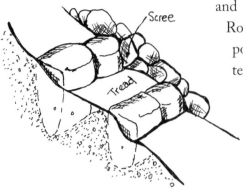

Small rocks can be set on edge and backfilled to build steps.

and mattocks to position the rock. Rock steps should not shift at any point, even slightly. Jump on it to test it; if it moves try repositioning it. Packing good, solid soil around it may help. Don't shim it with small rocks; they can work themselves loose. Sometimes a stubborn rock needs to be removed after you've placed it so you can improve the hole, or find a better rock. Proper rock-step placement requires skill, experience, and lots of hard work and patience.

When only small- and medium-sized rocks are available, several must be put side by side to provide a treadway of adequate width. When using thin, flat stones, place them on edge, buried deep in the trail tread and leaning back into the slope. Backfill the area behind and above the rock with soil and rubble. With an uphill lean, pressure from hikers' feet will push the rock into the slope rather than out and away from it.

On a steep slope, the rocks may need to be closely spaced, sometimes overlapping lower steps up to, or even more than, half their surface area. Overlapping large, flat rocks add stability to the other steps along the slope. Smaller rocks should not be used to

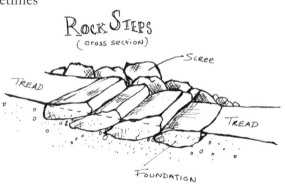

Overlapping large, flat rocks create stable steps.

"shim" a step that is unstable. Shims between rocks will eventually work loose and the step may fall out. Each rock should be solidly fitted into the soil and onto steps below. When using overlapping stones, two or more contact points are required for stability.

For aesthetic reasons, and in some cases to allow for better drainage, it is best to avoid building perfectly straight staircases up a slope. Nature is unruly, so put some twists and bends in the staircase if they don't affect stability. Also, drainage is easier to construct at the corners of the staircase. You can also break up the "staircase effect" through use of odd-shaped but well-placed rocks. Offset some steps rather than keep them in a direct line, and make sure that the placement doesn't impede a hiker's stride.

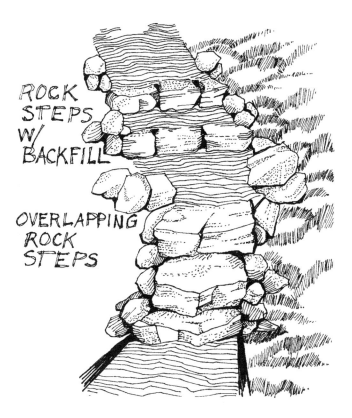

ROCK STEPS W/ BACKFILL

OVERLAPPING ROCK STEPS

Rock steps can also encourage hikers not to bypass steep, ledgy areas. These bypasses damage soils and vegetation along the sides of the ledge. Stack large rocks on top of each other and wedge them into any existing corners or cracks in the ledge. Although more difficult than setting steps in soil, secure and attractive footing can be built to help hikers gain a short ledge.

As with the entire trail, rock steps need drainage. Without it, even the largest, most stable steps will eventually work loose as the soil around them washes away. Ice will move steps too. Drainage, preferably rock water bars, should be installed above a series of steps. Plan for and put in rock water bars in the middle of long staircases. Take advantage of turns if possible.

Cleanup

After the rock work is completed brush in evidence of excavation and "skidder trails" and fill holes with debris, deadwood, and leaf litter, especially near the trail. Many heavily worked trails will look muddy or raw immediately after construction but will "wear in" over the course of a year or two. In this respect, rock work has an advantage over wood, since well-constructed rock work fits into the landscape.

Wood Steps

The construction of wood steps is for the most part similar to building wood water bars, except that steps are put

Use pin rocks to secure log steps and define the tread.

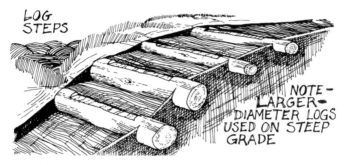

Wood steps must be longer than the width of the trail.

in perpendicular to the trail and the uphill side of the log is backfilled and not ditched.

Spruce and fir are, again, the usual choices for wood; the diameter should be between six and twelve inches. On steeper slopes a larger-diameter log gives more vertical rise. With small-diameter stock, steps have to be very close together and more numerous to provide the desired vertical rise. Peel the log if possible.

Wood steps should be longer than the width of the trail. When placed in a gully, the ends of the logs should extend into the banks. Too short a step will allow water and people to go around, and will not fully retain the soil.

To build a wood step, dig a trench with a depth roughly one-third the diameter of the log. Save the soil for backfill. Then set the log into the trench and secure it with pin rocks similar to those described for water bars earlier in this chapter.

Once the log step is secure, backfill the uphill side with the soil removed from the trench. When steps are placed in a series, the bottom of the upper log should be just a bit higher than the top of the lower log, with the soil in between sloped slightly downhill. This will prevent puddling behind the step. For a final touch, flatten the top of the log slightly with an ax to make a firm, flat tread.

Rock and Log Cribbing

Rock and *log cribbing* are techniques that involve creating a treadway along sections of trail that have been gullied by severe erosion or traverse a steep side slope.

Steps and water bars can repair a gully; but, in especially deep and wide gullies that are difficult to drain, they may not halt erosion. It may be better to remove the trail from the bottom of the gully onto the edge and support it with cribbing. On steep sidehill cuts, cribbing stabilizes the upper and lower slopes along the trail.

Rock cribbing, the most aesthetic and durable technique, is used to strengthen the low side of a trail. On steep sidehill locations the low side of a treadway must sometimes be built up as a rock wall. Start constructing the cribbing wall with a foundation of large rocks set deep into holes, sloped toward the bank, and tightly side by side for the length of the cribbing. Securely set layers of rock above these to the desired height. Additional layers of rock should overlapped and slightly behind the ones below. Therefore, each rock and the entire wall will lean into the bank toward the trail and be less likely to dislodge.

ROCK CRIB CROSS SECTION

Rock cribs support the lower edge of the treadway.

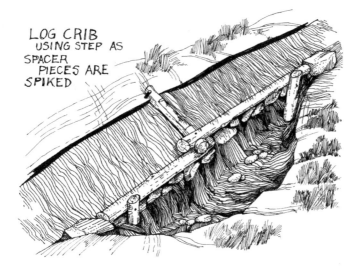

LOG CRIB
USING STEP AS
SPACER
    PIECES ARE
SPIKED

Log cribbing consists of one or more logs securely positioned alongside the edge of the trail. The logs should be at least ten inches in diameter and peeled. Length depends on the area, but generally long, heavy logs are best. The weight helps to hold the cribbing in place. The logs should be very secure, as they must support large amounts of soil and rock along with the weight of the passing hikers. Logs can be secured by large stakes or rocks, or butted up against rocks or trees. Logs set perpendicular to the trail—like a wood step—and notched and spiked into the crib logs can be used as combination steps, spacers, and retainers.

Fill gaps in the cribbing and build a treadway above with excavated rock and soil. The treadway above the cribbing should remain gently sloped to the outside or downhill side to ensure drainage. No cribbing should inhibit this drainage, nor should the treadway be flat or sloped toward the inside or uphill side of the treadway. Otherwise, water will puddle or flow along the tread.

After cribbing along the side of a gully, fill the gully with rock and wood debris to reduce further erosion and prevent access by hikers. Ideally, the gully will begin to fill with forest litter and will partially recover.

The uphill side of the tread can be strengthened by building a retaining wall that can be constructed in the same way as a rock or log cribbing. See illustration below.

Special Techniques—When placing steps is impossible, more complex structures such as log ladders, cribbed steps, or pinned steps may be necessary. This usually occurs in very steep locations or on bare ledges.

Log Ladder—This structure allows hikers to safely and comfortably ascend or descend a difficult ledge. Without it hikers may risk injury or bypass the difficult ledge, damaging adjacent soils and vegetation and further exposing the ledge. There are many variations of log ladders needed to suit the steepness and characteristics of each ledge. A basic design is described below, but the main components of a ladder are the stringers, the two long uprights, and the rungs (the log steps fastened in between the two stringers).

First measure the ledge to determine the length needed for the two stringers. Add a few feet to one or both of the stringers so a hiker has something to hang on to when standing on the top rung.

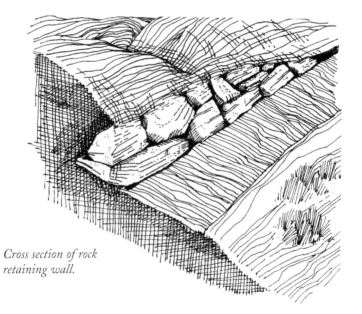

Cross section of rock retaining wall.

Cut, peel, and limb a matching pair of stringers from straight, sound trees eight to twelve inches in diameter. Put stringers into place leaving about eighteen to twenty-four inches between them and with larger, butt ends down. If there isn't a good, solid foundation for the butt ends, a base log should be used to support the stringers. Use a log equal or larger in diameter than the butt of the stringers, and at least a couple of feet longer than the distance between the outer edges of the stringers. Base logs may be cut longer to fit securely into par-

Log ladder under construction, showing long stringers with notches for rungs.

ticular features at the base of the ladder. Set the base log into a trench dug in the earth or fitted into gaps or cracks in the ledge. Cut a shallow, flat notch on top of the base log into which the bottoms of the stringer can be set. Then spike them into place. Top the base log to act as the first step.

THE RIGHT TOOLS: LOG LADDERS

- ax
- crosscut saw, bow saw, or chain saw
- large chisel and mallet
- hatchet (for shaping the log)

- tape measure, small level, crayon
- mattock and shovel
- sledgehammer (for driving spikes)
- 10–12 3/8-inch-diameter spikes

Lay out the placement of the notches along the inside of the stringers so the spacing from the top of one to the next is the same (about twelve to sixteen inches). Be sure the notches on the left are level with those on the right. The notches should be four-inch-deep and four-inch-wide dadoes, or three-side notches, with the tops and bottom sides flat, level, and parallel to each other. Saw the top and bottom sides first, then saw a few relief cuts in between and chisel out the remaining wood. Once a pair of notches is complete a rung can be cut and shaped to fit.

Cut rungs from six-to-eight-inch-diameter logs and top them to provide a stepping surface. Remove no more than one-quarter to one-third of the log. Measure the distance between the insides of the pair of notches and cut the rung to that length. Flatten the bottom ends of the rung parallel to the top to form a tongue four inches wide and a little more than four inches long to fit in the notches. Check the fit and fine-tune as needed to achieve a good, snug fit. Position the rung in the notches and spike by driving a spike through the stringers and into the ends of the rung. It's best to do one step at a time, starting at the bottom.

Crib Ladder—Another special stabilizer is a *crib ladder*, or a combination of cribbing and stepping. This technique is useful on a very

CRIB LADDER
RUNGS FIT INTO NOTCHES
AND ARE SPIKED
STEPS ARE BACKFILLED
WITH ROCK AND SCREE

steep slope or one with thin soil or bedrock near the surface of the ground, making it difficult to secure regular steps. Here you build a log ladder, lay it into or up against the slope, then backfill each step with soil and small rocks to help secure the slope. Do not leave gaps behind the rungs—people might step into them.

Pinned Steps—Local U.S. Forest Service staff have used wooden *pinned steps* to climb and traverse difficult ledges that do not provide adequate foot- and handholds and that cannot be avoided through relocation. Pressure-treated wooden steps two feet long are produced by ripping six-by-eight-inch stock diagonally from corner to corner. They are attached to the ledge with foot-long steel bars set partially into the rock. A gas-powered jackhammer is used to drill the holes. A jackhammer can also be used to cut steps into a

Treated wood steps secured to a rock face with steel pins.

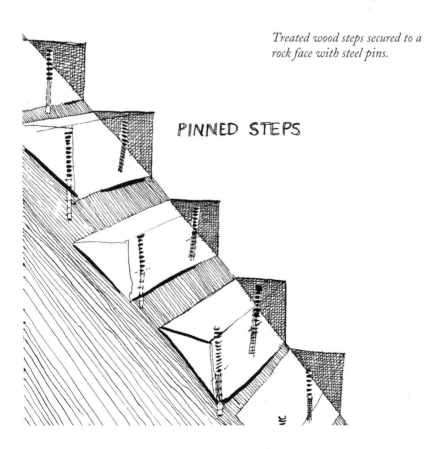

PINNED STEPS

ledge. Most maintainers agree that these high-standard techniques should be utilized only as a last resort to more-conventional work or relocation due to expense and difficulty, as well as aesthetics.

Hardeners

Hikers on trails in flat, low-lying, wet terrain, as well as mountain bogs with highly organic, wet soils, frequently cause destruction of bordering plants and surface soil. Wet, slippery, muddy spots develop very quickly on these soils. When water accumulates on the treadway, hikers walk to the side of the tread to keep their feet clean and dry. This causes a vicious circle of soil breakdown and trail widening. There are a number of techniques that "harden" the treadway and help to stabilize the damaged soils, allowing trailside plant life to recover.

Step stones, bog bridges, or built-up treadways are the most frequently used solutions in these situations. They are labor intensive and high impact, though. So before these techniques are used, drainage and relocation techniques should be considered first.

Drainage and Relocation

Wet, muddy locations frequently develop on trails because the treadway is lower than surrounding terrain. Water draining laterally through soils becomes trapped on the lower and compacted surfaces of the treadway. Rather than bridge or step-stone trails in these situations, drain the wet area in question—especially if it is small and has a low end that, once ditched, would permit water to flow off the trail. This is a better long-term solution. Often what initially appears to be a low, flat section of trail will actually have a very moderate slope, allowing an imperceptible flow of water. Drain small "flowing" wet spots such as this with water bars and drainage ditches. Installing drainages may not completely dry up the trail but can reduce the amount of hardening needed.

If an area cannot be drained, or if for environmental reasons it should not be drained, and if relocation is not feasible, then use trail-hardening techniques. These techniques offer dry passage for hikers and contain traffic on a hardened surface, allowing adjacent soils and plant life to reestablish themselves.

Step Stones and Rock Treadway

Again, where available and possible, rock is the best choice—for aesthetic reasons and durability.

Step stones

These are rocks set into the mud so that a stable, dry, and easily traversed treadway is formed. They can also be used to cross shallow streams. Step stones should have a flat stepping surface at least twelve inches across and should be thick enough to sit above the mud. Larger and flatter rocks will be easier to set and are less prone to unwanted movement than smaller, rounded ones. Present the flattest surface for walking by setting the stone in cone-shaped holes much like setting a rock step. Space them in line along the trail so a hiker with a heavy pack can easily stride from one to the next. Step stones should be stable and must not protrude too high above the ground or be so low as to be inundated with mud and water; otherwise, people are likely to avoid them.

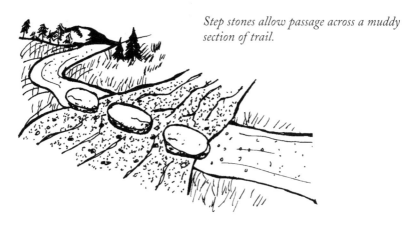

Step stones allow passage across a muddy section of trail.

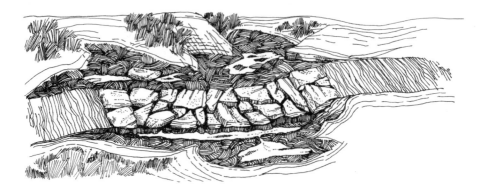

Rock treadway

Rock treadway

This is simply a more intensive use of rock than step stones. Many step-stone-size rocks are set side by side, covering the whole tread-way. Smaller and oddly shaped rocks, not useful for a rock treadway, can be set into a *rock box*. To make a rock box, construct a frame of logs, peeled, spiked together, and set halfway into the ground, then fill in the interior with rock. With particularly square rock a frame is not needed, since the rocks can be laid in flagstone fashion.

Turnpikes

Where an ample supply of good soil is available nearby, perimeters of rocks or log boxes can be made and filled, first with small rocks

ROCK BOX

Rock treadway is an effective and enduring way to harden a trail.

then capped with soil, to create a turnpike. These provide a nice walking surface, though the process is very time consuming. Another technique is to dig drainage ditches on one or both sides of the tread, using soil from the ditch excavation to build up the tread. Do not be afraid to use wet soil; it will dry out after a while.

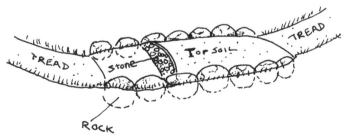

Cross section of a turnpike shows fill supported by stone and rock.

Bog Bridges

In areas where rock is scarce and mud is soft and deep, which is often the case in boggy locations, bog bridges, constructed of logs, form a hardened tread.

These bridges can also be used to ford small streams and gullies. In either case they will provide a dry, stable treadway. Such bridges usually last ten to fifteen years or more depending on species of tree, wetness of location, and diameter and quality of wood used. Softwoods such as cedar, hemlock, spruce, and fir are the easiest to work with and last the longest.

Bog bridges made of rough cut lumber can be flown in where native materials are scarce.

A bog bridge is generally made up of two eight- to twelve-foot-long, flat-topped logs called *stringers*, which form the walking surface. The stringers are supported near their ends on two *base logs* securely set into the surface of the mud. The stringers are fitted into notches in the base logs and spiked into place.

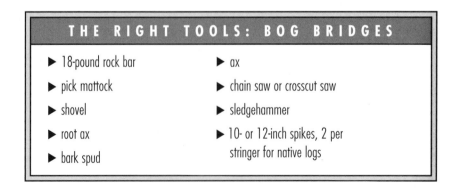

THE RIGHT TOOLS: BOG BRIDGES

- ▶ 18-pound rock bar
- ▶ pick mattock
- ▶ shovel
- ▶ root ax
- ▶ bark spud

- ▶ ax
- ▶ chain saw or crosscut saw
- ▶ sledgehammer
- ▶ 10- or 12-inch spikes, 2 per stringer for native logs

There are three types of log stringers for bog bridges: topped, split, and ripped. *Topped log* bridges are relatively simple to construct, requiring only a few hand tools (although a chain saw can help speed up the process). *Split* log bridges require the use of larger, higher-quality logs as well as additional tools and time. *Ripped* log bridges are similar to the split log but are made by sawing a log in half with a chain saw. This produces a flat surface but involves a great deal of wear and tear on the chain saw and the operator. A large chain saw with a ripping chain, requiring an experienced operator, is necessary.

Topped log bridges are the most durable, and therefore the best bridges to use. Because the stringers are topped and have no more than one-third of their mass removed, these bridges are stronger and more impervious to water and to rot than split or ripped log bridges. The stability gained from the extra weight of a topped log bridge is a positive characteristic.

Topped Log Bridges

A sharp ax is the one tool necessary to construct a topped log bridge. A crosscut saw may be helpful, and a small chain saw can make the work easier and faster. A peeler or bark spud facilitates peeling, and an adze can be used for topping. For driving spikes a sledgehammer is best, but the back of a root ax will do. Digging tools such as a mattock, shovel, and root ax are used for placing base logs.

Topped log bog bridge.

With smaller-diameter logs used for topped log bridge stringers, two are needed side by side to provide a treadway of adequate width. Stringers should be eight to ten inches in diameter. Shorter bridges can have stringers as narrow as six inches in diameter at their thinnest end. Length is usually from eight to twelve feet, as longer spans tend to be springy and may break. Base logs should be three to four feet long and eight to ten inches in diameter. Where it is extremely wet and mud is soft and deep, larger and longer base logs may be necessary for stability and better flotation. Logs should be peeled to retard rot and be easier to work with.

Installation

Building a log bridge is best done in pairs, one working on each end of the bridge and helping each other to move the logs. The first step in bridging a boggy section of trail is to determine the length of the bridge or bridges needed. If a series of bridges is needed, divide up the entire length so each bridge averages the same length between eight and twelve feet. Often large rocks, roots, and trees will dictate where bridges can be placed and determining their lengths. In any case, construct one brigde at a time, starting at one edge of the muddy section and working your way across to achieve proper spacing and placement. A tape measure works best but a length of rope or counting ax lengths will also work.

A series of correctly spaced bog bridges.

Once you've measured the length of the bridge the next step is to find appropriate trees for the bridge parts. Don't waste wood by using a tree that is too long for a bridge part (see chapter 6). Trees should be straight, have few branches, and be free of defects. Be sure to cut logs so each pair of stringers is closely matched in size and shape. Take the time to find good-quality wood; it will save time and effort during construction and make for a better, longer-lasting bridge. Cut to length, limb, and peel logs away from the trail so the debris stays out of sight. The two base logs and pair of stringers can then be brought to the trail and laid in place.

Now the base logs can be positioned and set into place. To gauge their placement lay out one stringer along the center of the treadway on the surface of the mud. Make sure it is no more than six inches from solid treadway, step stone, or another bridge. Mark the position for the base logs so that they are perpendicular to the stringers and so the stringers overhang the base logs at their centers by no more than six inches. Too much overhang can break off or tip up the bridge when it is stepped on. Move the stringer aside and dig a trench to fit each of the base logs. The trenches should be as wide and long as the base logs and about as deep as one-half the logs' diameter. The base logs need to be level and secure; check this by stomping on both ends. It may be necessary to remove roots and small rocks to properly place the base logs.

The next step is to lay out the two stringers on the base logs. Alternate the butt, thicker, ends to achieve a uniform width. For greater strength, rotate the stringers so any slight crown, or curve, is up, higher in the center than the ends. Position the pair so they fit closely together along their entire length but with a small gap still remaining for drainage. The gap between the stringers should be no more than one to two inches so a foot cannot slip down between them. Once the ideal layout is determined, mark the stringers' tops and also sides where they line up with the base logs so they can be repositioned correctly during construction.

With the stringers in position the placement of the notches in the base logs can now be marked. Draw a line with a pencil or ax on the top of the base log parallel to and straight down along both sides of the stringers. Move the stringers to the side and chop or saw out a 90-degree, V-shaped notch between the lines. Be careful not to make the notches too large at first; they can always be made larger but never smaller. Start with slightly undersized notches, check the fit and fine-tune them as needed. The sides of the stringers should fit neatly along the sides of the notches and not rest on the bottom, pinching them in place. To get the tops of two stringers at the same level, widen the notch of the higher or larger stringer to set it lower. When the stringers are finally fitted in the notches their bottoms should be just touching the surface of the mud.

The stringers can now be topped flat, level, and even with each other to provide a walking surface. Remove only one-quarter to one-third of the logs; this will still be wide enough for walking without decreasing the strength more than necessary. This can be done with an ax alone or by first sawing relief cuts at six-inch intervals with a crosscut or chain saw and then chipping out the sections with an ax or adze. Be sure to clean up the chips and scatter them off the trail.

Make four- to six-inch relief cuts with saw and top.

End view showing stringers fitted into notches and secured with spikes. Longer base logs increase stability.

The final step is to spike the stringers to the base logs. Use ten- to twelve-inch-long, 3/8-inch spikes. Drive them in with a sledge-hammer or the back side of a root ax. Strike them squarely. A bent-over spike is extremely difficult to remove.

Slightly angle the spikes so they pass through the stringers and into the side of the notch. Angle the spikes in opposite directions at each end to provide tension to hold the stringers more securely in place.

Bridge Construction Reminders

- Whether you build a split log or topped log bridge, in order for it to be effective it must be used by the hiker. Make sure that the treadway width is sufficient to make walking on it easy. In some cases it may be necessary to use double stringers, two side by side—or in the case of particularly thin stock, three in parallel.

- The treadway should not be tilted or angled to one side, nor should the bridge be unstable, rocking, or very springy. For stringers that are more than eight-to ten-feet long or that are very springy, use three or more base logs for support. It is probably best to keep bridges short and therefore stable. Shorter bridges are also easier to work with.

- The height of the bridge surface should not be over eight to ten inches from the ground. A high bridge is hard to step up onto or off of, and can be difficult to traverse for those averse to heights. Dig in the base logs if the unit will be too high or if it is unstable.

- Also, a stable rocky or dry soil should be found at the end of a bridge, not mud or slippery roots. When bridges are placed end to end, a space of no more than six inches should separate them.

- Caution should be exercised when building bridges on pond shores or in any areas that are prone to flooding in wet seasons. If water levels rise substantially, bridges will float and drift off the trail. This might happen, for instance, along a pond shore that has beaver activity. Trails in these situations might best be relocated rather than bridged.

Definers

Over time many hikers using the same shortcuts create bootleg or social trails. People tend to seek the path of least resistance. To save time and effort hikers will cut corners at switchbacks, walk on the smooth carpet of alpine vegetation, or go around rock steps. Hikers who stray off a trail will quickly trample vegetation, compact soils, and hasten trailside erosion. Even a well-marked and maintained trail may need further defining. Place definers to make walking off the trail difficult, thus containing traffic to a single stabilized treadway.

Scree Walls

Low, simple rows of small rocks, called *scree walls*, lining the edges of the trail clearly show the boundaries of the trail and act as an impediment to straying hikers. Scree walls are often needed along-

SCREE WALLS

.Scree walls were constructed in 1977 to minimize hiker impact on alpine vegetation on Franconia Ridge, N.H. The scree walls were effective in protecting alpine habitat from hiker trampling and in permitting natural revegetation. Hair cap moss (*Polytricum juniperinum* var. *alpestre*) and mountain sandwort (*Minuartia groenlandica*) dominated revegetation

of the disturbed areas. Scree walls create a protective microhabitat for alpine vegetation. Questionnaire results showed 87 percent of the hikers felt the scree walls effective and 80 percent felt them unobtrusive.

Well-maintained rock cairns, paint marks, and educational signs complement the scree walls. The removal of rock for scree wall construction must be done selectively. Scree walls offer excellent long-term passive trail management with minimal annual cost.

—From *Passive Trail Management in Northeastern Alpine Zones: A Case Study*, J. D. Doucette and K. D. Kimball, Proceedings of the Northeastern Recreation Research Symposium, 1990.

Photos show comparison of trail transect #58 on Franconia Ridge in 1975 without scree wall (top) and with scree walls in 1989 (bottom). Note revegetation in 1989 photo.

*Scree walls define the treadway and protect
fragile alpine vegetation.*

side heavily used trails in open alpine zones. Always line rock steps
with scree walls; bypassed edges of steps will soon erode and threat-
en the stability of the steps and the entire slope. Scree is also used
to block the shortcutting of switchbacks and to keep hikers from
going around water bars or into drainage ditches.

Use small- to medium-size rocks that can be carried by one person. Set scree so it can't be kicked or knocked out by someone walking on it. Toppled walls and loose rocks in the trail won't help the
situation. Securely set scree is particularly important along rock

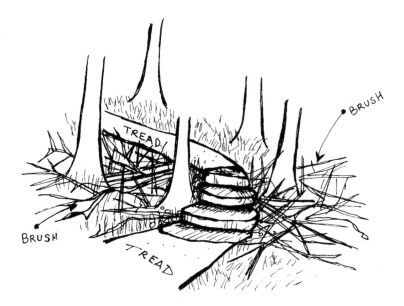

Use dead brush and logs to keep hikers on the trail and discourage shortcutting.

steps because scree also serves to stabilize the soil. Scree walls should only be as large as they need to be, though substantial walls are needed where hikers regularly walk off the trail. The maintainer should recognize that scree walls can greatly infringe on the primitive qualities of the trail environment. Strive to make these scree walls as unobtrusive and natural appearing as possible.

Rubble

To help widened sections of trail outside the scree wall recover from damage, scatter *rubble* over the area. Walking on a jumble of small, loose stones is no fun and should keep people on the trail. Rubble is also an effective way to close a bootleg trail.

Brush

In scrubby and wooded areas, dead brush and logs are useful for narrowing trails, protecting switchbacks, and closing unwanted trails. Remember that this brush will eventually rot away, but it will allow time for plants and trees to start growing back.

CHAPTER EIGHT
Bridges and Stiles

While rock is the preferred material for most trail construction, it is not ideal for everything. Sooner or later, you'll need to build something on your trail out of wood, and that something is likely to be a bridge, or stile. These structures are more complicated than a simple bog bridge or log water bar, and can be made out of native or milled lumber.

Bridges

Almost all trails, somewhere in their route, cross one or more streams. Hiker safety is the primary consideration when determining need for a bridge, but convenience and challenge are also important factors. For example, hopping from stone to stone and the possibility of getting wet feet are part of the backcountry experience. On the other hand, convenience may be important on an urban nature trail used by a wide variety of people, many in street shoes and with little hiking experience.

In April 1995, the Board of Managers of the Appalachian Trail Conference adopted the following policy on the construction or replacement of bridges on the Appalachian Trail:

A bridge should be constructed or replaced only if:

1. It is essential to hiker safety during the snow-free hiking season, recognizing that a stream may be unfordable when seasonal or regular flooding occurs; or

2. It is absolutely necessary to protect sensitive resources such as soils along a river's bank.

A trail crossing that does not require a bridge in the summer for hikers may need one for skiers in the winter. Requirements during normal low-stream flows may be quite different from those during spring thaw. Some streams are also prone to unexpected flash floods, when water levels and currents will change dramatically; in such cases a bridge may be required.

Before bridging larger streams, be certain the crossing is necessary. Sometimes a crossing can be eliminated through a different trail route. If a crossing must be made, determine whether or not the present location is the best one. Look up- and downstream for a ford or a crossing requiring a smaller bridge. Avoid areas with eroded banks. Straighter stretches of stream are the most stable; stream bends tend to erode at the outside.

Natural stream crossings or fords are best. Use large step stones where stream flow is low and does not greatly fluctuate; otherwise, the step stones will be submerged or washed away. Also, the stream bottom must be solid for this crossing method to be effective.

Depending on where you are, bridges over certain lengths and heights require a permit from the local jurisdiction. Most activities involving soil disturbance in a stream bed or along its banks require wetlands permits. Complete your paperwork once you've decided on a crossing and a bridge design.

For small stream crossings of ten to fifteen feet in width, a simple log puncheon or bog bridge (see chapter 7) may suffice. For stream crossings, use a bridge with double stringers to provide better footing. Build a handrail for bridges three feet or higher above the stream or those over a fast current.

Determine flood levels in advance. Look for evidence of the high-water mark in the form of scraped bark on stream bank trees and deposits of stream debris. Consult local residents for observations and the Natural Resource Conservation Service or the town clerk for stream flow and flood-level data. In some cases an existing flood overflow channel will need to be spanned by a larger bridge or extension to avoid loss of the bridge.

Building Single-Span Stringer Bridges

Single-span wooden bridges of native materials or milled timber are the most common large bridges on trails. If both stream banks are high enough to keep the stringers well above the flood level, extensive cribbing is not necessary. Secure the stringers to a single base log or sill on each end, using 10- or 12-inch spikes or large bolts. Place the base log on a flat stone or ledge to prevent rot; the base log should not directly contact soil if at all possible. Drift pins can be used to hold the base log in place if the weight of the bridge itself is not sufficient.

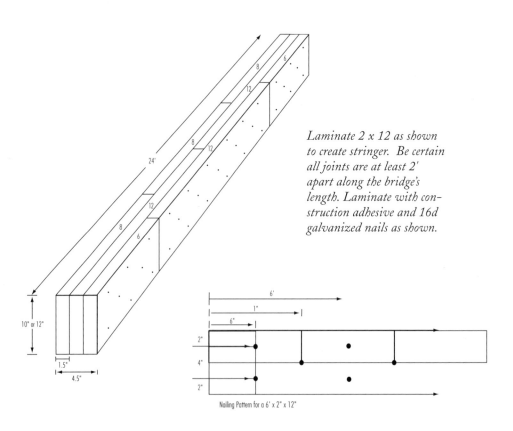

Laminate 2 x 12 as shown to create stringer. Be certain all joints are at least 2' apart along the bridge's length. Laminate with construction adhesive and 16d galvanized nails as shown.

Nailing Pattern for a 6' x 2" x 12"

TWO STRINGER WITH RAIL

Dimensional, pressure-treated lumber can be used to build simple and durable triple-laminated bridge stringer for spans up to 24 feet. Laminated stringers are created by joining sections of 2 x 12 together in three layers to form one solid beam. Before laminating, each section of 2 x 12 should be checked for bows, and bowed sections should be positioned crown up, to take advantage of the bow's strength. Laminate the 2 x 12s together using both galvanized nails (as shown in the diagram) and construction adhesive for maximum strength. Joints between laminated sections should never be closer than 2 feet to each other. Two-by-tens may be used to create stringers up to 12 feet long.

For bridges made of native materials, use rot-resistant wood such as hemlock, locust, spruce, larch, or Douglas fir for the entire bridge including the base logs. Remove all bark. If you feel the bridge should be treated to retard rot, use pressure-treated wood or treat the native wood with borax. Use liquid wood treatments with extreme caution; while they can lengthen the life of the bridge, their ingredients are often toxic and may leach into the stream. Should you use such a treatment, dry the logs before application and apply the treatment on dry ground to keep the liquid preservative out of the stream.

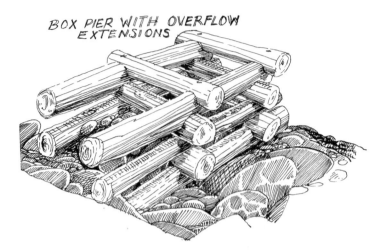

BOX PIER WITH OVERFLOW
EXTENSIONS

Sometimes one stream bank is low and a crib is needed to get the bridge high enough at one end so that the bridge is level. In other locations, cribs or piers may be necessary at both ends. Stone piers are more durable than log cribs, but they require a great deal of effort and the skill of a mason and they may be out of place in some settings. *Gabions*, wire cages filled with stone, can be used instead of piers. Log cribs are most commonly used.

Construct wood cribs of logs 8 to 10 inches in diameter. Cut notches with an ax or chain saw on the underside of each log to prevent water from collecting. Use drift pins or 10-to-12-inch 3/8-inch-diameter spikes to hold the logs together.

To add mass and strength, fill the crib with rock gathered nearby or from the stream as you construct it. Be aware that removing stones from the stream channel may change water flow, and such work almost always requires a permit. Larger rocks can be pushed or pulled to each side of the stream and placed along the bases of the cribs, particularly on the upstream side, for added protection. Use string or squared-off, milled lumber and a builder's level to get the two cribs the same height.

After the crib has been built high enough, secure the stringer to it using large spikes or galvanized bolts. The size of the stringer will depend upon the type of wood and length of the span.

Due to their length and weight, stringers are hard to carry and maneuver into position. Timber carriers, hand winches with extra lengths of cable or chain, and crowbars can greatly facilitate the task. Place small lengths of log underneath stringers to provide rollers. Horses or small tractors might be used in easily accessible locations. When you get the stringer to the site, place it across the stream, with the ends beside each sill or crib; then lift it into place. Ramps made of logs and placed against the side of a crib can help get the stringer up on top. Again, check the bridge's length and width with the carpenter's level.

Decking, made from small-diameter (4 to 6 inches) logs, larger logs split in half, or rough-cut timber two inches thick, goes on next. Avoid pressure-treated wood for a foot surface on sloped bridges or in areas that don't dry out—it is extremely slippery when wet. Should you use such wood, use a surface treatment to enhance traction. It is possible simply to have two or more stringers, hewn or adzed flat on the top for good footing, to provide an adequate

Three-stringer bridge with rail.

Pressure-treated bridge with stringers and railing.

treadway, if the stringers are close together. Generally, though, decking is best. Small spaces, 1/4 inch to 3/4 inch wide, should be left between deck pieces to allow for drainage. Before putting decking on, place tar paper or aluminum flashing over the top of the stringers for drainage and to help prevent rot. If the bridge is over a fast current or three feet or more above the stream, add a secure railing to one or both sides. In some cases, steps or a small ladder are required on each end due to the height of the cribs. Where access is easy and the use of nonnative material is appropriate (for example, on a high-use trail close to a road), pressure-treated telephone poles can be used for stringers. Pressure-treated lumber can also be used for the decking and railings.

To prevent the complete loss of the bridge during floods, cable one end of the stringers to a large tree, boulder, or other anchor upstream. If washed loose, one end will float free and the bridge will end up against the stream bank more or less intact. Later, the bridge can be put back, or at least taken apart and reassembled in its place. If you cable both sides, the bridge may stay in place but collect debris and eventually succumb completely to the force of the flood. Do not underestimate the power of a flooding stream.

Other Designs

The load capacity of fixed stringers generally limits spans to forty feet or less. A longer distance can be bridged using a midstream center crib and two spans. This will work only where flood levels are low and flow is slow; otherwise, the center crib may be destroyed.

BRIDGE WITH FLOOD-
LEVEL EXTENSION

Most stream crossings of forty feet or more require specially designed bridges such as a laminated timber bridge (10 to 60'), a prefabricated steel bridge (20 to 168 feet), a web joist bridge (about 100 feet), or a timber suspension bridge (up to 200 feet). These are all extremely expensive, ranging in total cost from $20,000 to $150,000. They also require the expertise of engineers and experienced builders to install them.

Where stream crossings are large and unavoidable, requiring an expensive bridge, be sure an existing trail or road bridge nearby can-

Bridge with center crib.

TENSION BRIDGE

not be utilized. Sometimes it is best to consider relocating a trail rather than tackle such a large, expensive project.

Truss Bridges

If you are interested in history and wish to build a bridge (other than a native log style) that is similar in nature to the trail, consider a kingpost, queenpost, or other type of truss bridge. These earlier ancestors of the well-known covered bridge work well with spans from fifteen to seventy-five feet.

The original kingpost trusses were prone to ice and flood damage, since they were underneath the stringers. Eventually

Pressure-treated bridge with triple-laminated stringers and railing.

someone realized that the principle of the triangle, which will hold its shape under pressure, would work just as well on top of the bridge. The queenpost design allowed a longer span and more complex designs using multiple trusses and arches to further lengthen the distance that could be bridged. Research the history of covered bridges if you are interested. For the mortise and tenon joints commonly used, look into one of the many good books available on post and beam construction.

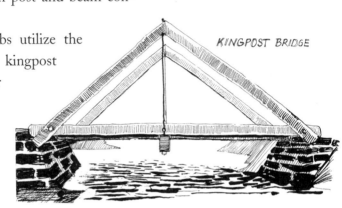

KINGPOST BRIDGE

Some trail clubs utilize the principle of the kingpost bridge in their designs, often using a combination of native logs and cable. Another version uses a cable underneath the bridge to strengthen long stringers.

Special Stream-Crossing Devices

Cableways can be used for stream crossings as an alternative to bridging. In a few places small cable cars capable of carrying one person can be found. The hiker hops in, grabs a secondary cable, and pulls herself/himself across. A second hiker pulls back the car and repeats the process. In other situations, two cables are simply spaced one above the other and the hikers, with feet on the lower one and hands on the upper, slide-step across. Neither system is easy to use for most people, especially if there are large packs or young children and pets.

Where large bodies of water must be crossed, bridges built on pilings may be the answer. Floating bridges like life rafts and docks can be constructed using foam blocks, but they will need to be removed during the winter. Anchor cables should be placed to keep such a bridge stable and in position. Use rot-resistant wood, and make sure all hardware is galvanized or plated. Consult a local dock builder for advice on pilings and Styrofoam.

Planning for Other Uses

If your trail is only for hiking, build your bridge accordingly to prevent prohibited uses that may include snowmobiles or trail bikes. Build narrow bridges or place barricades at each end of the bridge to prevent undesirable use. Gates or stiles may also be used to prevent access to the bridge, and are particularly effective for keeping out farm animals. If the bridge is to be used by motor vehicles or animals, be certain to plan the carrying capacity of the bridge and its structure with more weight in mind.

Suspension bridges that are easily accessible or located near the roadside need extra anti-sway cables attached to each side. Groups of children may try to make the bridge flex up and down and from side to side. While it may sometimes be advantageous to have a high-visibility bridge, at other times the use of landscaping and planting to hide the bridge may be more desirable.

Assistance

The U.S. Forest Service has the most experience with and information on various designs of trail bridges. The National Park Service and state parks may also be able to provide advice. Local engineers, contractors, and utility companies may be able to give guidance or provide hardware and cable. Sometimes local National Guard units are willing to take on public service projects and can offer labor in addition to technical help. Check with other trail clubs and trail bike and snowmobile organizations for information.

Maintenance

Make an annual inspection of all bridges and stream crossings. Perform regular maintenance and replace materials as needed. Check all wood for soundness and paint or treat with preservative if required (take particular care to protect the water). Fix loose decking and railings. Have a qualified engineer perform the annual inspection on suspension or engineered bridges or any bridge that would likely cause serious injury should it fail. Paint any cables, steel beams, or hardware with rust-resistant paint. Keep a blueprint and pictures of each structure on file to aid repair work.

Stiles

Trails traversing private lands and agricultural areas sometimes pass over or through fences. Construct a stile to prevent damage to fences and to avoid conflict with the landowner over the inevitable gate that someone forgot to close. Stiles allow pedestrian travel and in most cases prevent passage of farm animals and unauthorized use by vehicles.

There are two types of lumber you can use for stile construction: milled and native.

Milled Lumber. You can use milled lumber to construct stiles in easily reached locations or where native materials are scarce or absent. With milled lumber, use two-inch or larger stock for strength. Rough-cut lumber has slightly larger dimensions than fully milled lumber and is strongest. Paint or treat the wood with preservative to ensure durability, but be certain to use nontoxic formulas that won't hurt animals. Treat railings or parts touched by hikers with preservatives that will not stain or burn. All nails, bolts, and hardware should be plated or galvanized.

Native Lumber. If you want a more rustic appearance and are up to the added challenge of working with native logs, it is possible to make stiles completely out of native materials. This is preferable at remote locations where native lumber is abundant and where it would be too difficult to import finished materials. Use rot-resistant tree species such as hemlock, spruce, cedar, or locust. Remove bark and treat any portions of logs buried in the ground with wood preservative to prevent rot.

Cover sections of electrified fence near stiles with a piece of rubber hose to protect hikers. Slit it the entire length and slip it over the wire. Use hose to cover exposed barbed wire that hikers might get caught on when crossing stiles.

Illustrated below are several common stile designs.

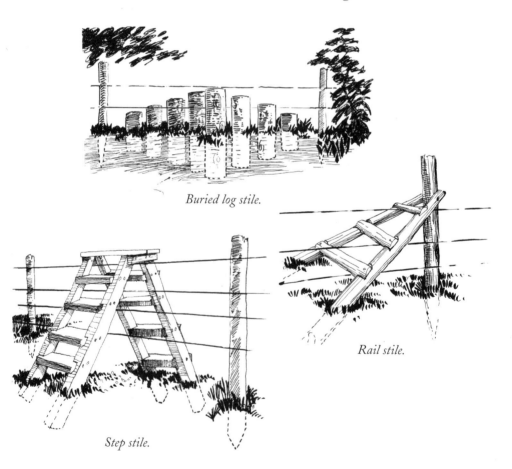

Buried log stile.

Rail stile.

Step stile.

Use a turnstile or walk-through stile to get hikers through a fence instead of over it. Where farm animals might go under or through a turnstile, use a walk-through stile; the tight turn and narrow space will keep most farm animals from getting through. To contain smaller farm animals, place a low step, barrier board, or hinged gate in the middle.

With stone walls, make a narrow opening for hikers. A stone staircase up one side and down the other can be built but requires a great deal more work.

Turnstile.

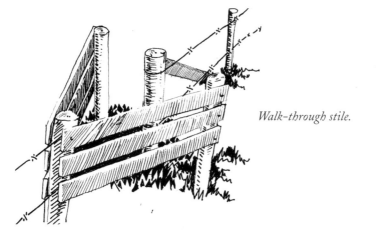

Walk-through stile.

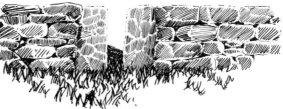

Stone wall stile.

CHAPTER NINE
Cross-Country Ski Touring Trails

S ki touring, also known as cross-country skiing, is great exercise, fun, relatively inexpensive, and more popular than ever.
Classical skiing and skate skiing on groomed trails at cross-country
ski areas continue to grow in popularity; however, over the last
ten years, backcountry (or telemark) skiing on ungroomed trails or
areas without trails has skyrocketed in popularity. More people are
discovering the challenge of backcountry skiing. The equipment
companies have responded by offering a wide selection of free-
heel skis with metal edges designed for every possible condition.
The telemark boots are sturdier than classic cross-country boots;

the bindings used are often simple cable bindings or a beefier version of the classic cross-country three pin. With the free heel, telemark skiers can ascend slopes or trails by using climbing skins or sticky wax on their skis. Opportunities for backcountry touring are widespread and exist in all degrees of difficulty, from a ski out through the backwoods lot to a major mountaineering trip into remote wildlands.

At the other end of the spectrum is competitive and recreational skiing and ski skating on developed, mechanically tracked, high standard trails. The private sector has worked hard to meet the demands for this kind of cross-country skiing, and the number of private touring centers on both private and public lands continues to grow.

In between is recreational touring on ungroomed primitive trails. As ski tourers become more experienced and skilled, some seek the challenging, less-used primitive trails. Even though these skiers aren't necessarily looking for grooming and set tracks, they do need clearly marked, brushed, and easily followed trails. Such a trail could range from an old fire road with a nice fall line to a blazed, brushed, specially constructed backcountry ski trail through dense woods.

A WORD ON TRACKS

Whether mechanically set by machinery or by skiers, tracks are often a precious commodity on ski trails, especially on backcountry trails with little or no grade. Tracks stabilize the skis so that skiers may concentrate on propelling themselves forward rather than keeping their skis straight while they break trail. Tracks are fragile and can easily be destroyed by snowmobiles, dogs, sleds, snowshoes, hikers, or discourteous skiers. Stay off them if you aren't on skis! After a new snow and a first grooming or use, tracks will take a couple of hours to set up before they provide maximum firmness and durability.

The Appalachian Mountain Club Trails Program maintains approximately twenty miles of ski touring trails in the Pinkham Notch area of the White Mountains. Other touring trails are maintained by chapters and camps of the club. All are free, ungroomed, and unpatrolled. The club supports these primitive ski touring opportunities as part of a spectrum of backcountry experiences.

Planning and Design

Development of a cross-country ski trail system should begin with a determination of the users' experience level, expected number of users, and whether or not it will be weekend use, day use, or evening use. Review chapters 2, 3, and 4 of this book for an overview of the applicable elements of hiking trail design.

Decide whether the maintaining organization will cater to one type of ski touring experience and level of expertise or to all. To some extent the land base will affect this decision. For instance, rough terrain might eliminate the possibility of building novice trails, while flat terrain may be unlikely to attract more-experienced backcountry skiers.

Use the standard trail degree-of-difficulty ratings noted here. The ratings are determined by trail gradient, alignment, and width, assessed during normal or average snow conditions. A ski touring system should ideally have approximately 50 percent of the trails rated as easiest for novice use; approximately 30 percent with a more difficult rating for intermediate skiers; and 20 percent most difficult trails for expert skiers. Trail location, terrain, and land management goals and objectives will affect these percentages.

Assess the other ski touring opportunities in the region to see if there is a niche you can fill, and investigate opportunities to connect with existing trails or areas to provide a larger network.

Take the time to evaluate other recreational activities and land management practices in the area. Watch for those that might pose conflicts, and minimize problems through trail layout and design. For example, snowmobiles and cross-country skiers are generally incompatible groups and should be separated for reasons of aesthetics and safety. Check to be sure timber management activities don't pose a problem; skid or wooded roads that are perfect for skiing can be heavily used by skidders and logging trucks during the winter harvest.

Review public accessibility thoroughly. Consider existing and potential roads, parking, public transportation, and winter snow removal. Design roads and parking areas to facilitate easy, efficient snow removal, and coordinate your snow removal activities with your local highway authorities or municipality.

Once you've figured out who your clientele will be, you'll need to determine how (or if) they will be provided with information and education. You should also consider sanitation facilities; search-and-rescue operations; and skier conveniences such as ski rental and repair, food, and lodging and meal accommodations. And don't forget management and maintenance of the trails too.

Assess your opportunities for expansion, and consider possibilities for future changes in operations, like the addition of warming shelters or grooming. Construction should allow for the possibility of operational changes. For instance, if you are planning on grooming in the future, design your trail system and corridors to allow grooming in on one trail and out on another. Construct your bridges to allow for the passage of grooming equipment.

Trail Layout

The best time to lay out ski touring trails is in the late fall or winter when leaves are off the trees and visibility is good. Before venturing out, consult maps and aerial photos to get a feel for the lay of the land and location of features. Remember the general trail layout considerations outlined in chapter 3 and the factors specific to ski touring described here.

Lay out the trail on skis in the winter; it's fun and the most effective way to actually test the "skiability" of the route. You can mark the route by your tracks and brightly colored flagging tape that stands out well against snow. Look out for the usual hazards—brush sticking out of the snow, hanging tree limbs, tree wells, and "spruce traps" that have snow on top and air and branches underneath.

Scout the route with another person to get a different perspective. Two or more people can also cover more ground. Cover the area several times before you focus on a particular route; you might find a natural feature like a ravine, nice forest area, some interesting ledges, or an old logging road that would be good to include on the trail. Walk or ski, uphill and downhill, a route in both directions to thoroughly assess its suitability.

Start your trail at an existing trailhead facility (like the parking area for a hiking trail) to allow for optimum use and to cut costs. Any new parking facility should be capable of handling likely use levels safely. Since they'll be used in winter, entrances to parking areas should not be steep or narrow, or have poor visibility. Ability to remove snow easily from parking facilities is also important.

Look for opportunities to use existing trails or roads for hikers, horseback riders, or summer off-road vehicles. Some trails or roads may be unusable for ski touring because of bog bridges, water bars, or drainage dips. Without sufficient snow cover, bog bridges stick up through the snow to create obstacles to skiers, and water bars and drainage dips form open, snowless gullies if the water in them does not freeze. Hiking trails may not be wide enough to safely accommodate skiing, particularly on slopes. Widening them sufficiently might destroy their appeal to hikers.

The best formats for ski touring trail layout are single loops, compound or stacked loops, or mazes, and variations on them. These configurations allow skiers to travel over several trail sections, cover variable distances, and return in the end to the same

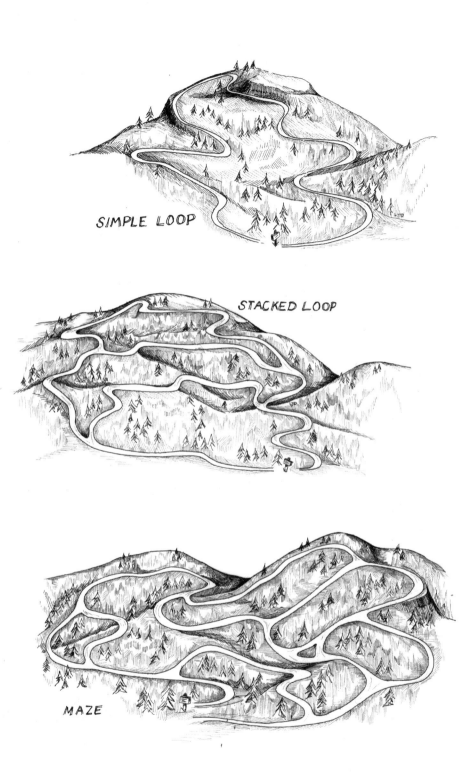

SIMPLE LOOP

STACKED LOOP

MAZE

starting point. A series of loops with various levels of difficulty will serve a wide range of skier abilities.

Use a one-way traffic policy on steep trails, places where collisions are likely, or heavily used loops. One-way traffic reduces congestion and provides a greater sense of solitude for the skier.

Straight-line trails between two points are desirable for connecting two ski touring systems or going from one inn to another. Some ski touring trails in New Hampshire's White Mountains leave the top of an alpine ski area and are downhill runs for their entire length to the valley below. Sometimes terrain or landowner limitations prevent development of loop trails to and from a natural feature or facility; if this is the case, use a straight single trail that must be backtracked to the starting point.

Location Considerations

Ski touring trail needs lots of snow. Review climatological data for the area to determine if your trail can receive sufficient snow coverage. The facings of slopes and type and quality of vegetation are important factors. Snow on south- and west-facing slopes gets more exposure to the sun, so will melt and evaporate faster. Sparse vegetation results in poor snow retention, and the wind and sun take their toll on both snow and skier. Favor north or east slopes and areas of denser vegetation—the latter particularly if a south or west slope must be traversed, since the snow cover will be shaded from the sun. The branches of dense softwood stands hold much of the snow off the ground, creating less snow coverage. And, since snow in the trees gets exposed to the sun, it melts and drops onto the trail, creating more icy conditions than on a trail through a hardwood or mixed stand.

Avoid areas of known avalanche danger and hazardous crossings of lakes, ponds, and streams. Bypass critical wildlife habitats. Strive to avoid or minimize conflicts with other winter recreationists, such as snowmobilers, by separating the paths used and providing adequate visual and sound buffers. Avoid hazardous crossings of busy roads. Road crossings or trails closely paralleling roads should also be avoided; they can be distracting and noisy. Avoid fences too; they are hazardous when near downhill runs and are difficult to cross.

Avoid boggy or wet areas, since springs and seepage may freeze late and open up early (if they freeze at all), leaving the trail impassable. Stream crossings that must be crossed without a bridge should have easy, gentle access. If a bridge is desired or necessary, stream banks should be high, stable, and as close together as possible to provide for secure bridge bases and to keep span length to a minimum.

Undulating terrain provides a varied ski touring experience. Smooth trails require the least amount of snowfall, so look for old logging roads, railroad beds, and naturally occurring terraces and benches for a smooth run. Avoid very rough terrain since it needs lots of snow to be skiable. Also avoid long, steep sidehill traverses where under icy conditions a skier may lose control and slide downhill. Grooming may be difficult, if not impossible, on steep sidehills. Sidehill traverses, in general, are often awkward and tiring because they demand that one ski be lower than the other. On the other hand, long, straight stretches of trail are usually very boring and allow skiers to build up excessive speed. Find a middle ground where the trail is not overly sinuous or too straight.

Construction

Many of the techniques and tools used in hiking trail construction apply to ski touring trails, but there are some specialized trail standards and techniques you should know.

Trail Width—The width of a ski touring trail depends on the type and amount of use, the slope, and trail layout. Developed, high-standard trails that are to be groomed require a wide trail (10 to 12 feet or more) to allow for grooming machinery. The width allows for the setting of two tracks. A moderate-use trail designed to have one set track could be 8 to 10 feet wide, and a low-use groomed trail could be as narrow as 4 to 6 feet wide. Slope affects width because of the need to snowplow while going downhill or to herringbone to get uphill; sloping trails should be at least 8 to 10 feet wide on an ungroomed trail. On corners, cut the trail wider to allow for turning and snowplowing. If you must (due to terrain), build a sharp turn.

When cutting brush to create the trail, cut stumps as flush with the ground as possible and trim limbs flush with tree trunks. Don't leave any hazardous protruding, sharp stumps or limbs.

Height—Remove branches to a height of 7 to 8 feet above the highest level of snow cover. Prune evergreen limbs higher since they tend to droop under the weight of snow.

Trail Tread—As noted earlier, the smoother the trail tread, the sooner the trail can be used and the longer the skiing season will last. You'll need to remove large rocks, cut stumps flush, and avoid unreasonably rough terrain and boulder fields.

More commercial ski touring areas are building high-standard ski touring trails that permit other recreational use during the snow-free part of the year. The trail base is smoothed and slightly crowned in the middle to allow for drainage. Drainage devices are installed alongside and underneath the trail, and the top is sometimes capped with a layer of wood chips or gravel. Large machinery is used and the relative cost is high, but a very durable, low-maintenance tread is the result. It can be skied on with very little snow cover, and in the summer, hikers, joggers, mountain bike riders, and horseback riders can enjoy it.

During construction, seed or mulch to stabilize the soil where sidehill cuts or the tread disturbs the ground cover. On traverses of steep sidehills, cut and fill the sidehill to create a terrace that will hold snow and provide a level tread. The placement of logs and

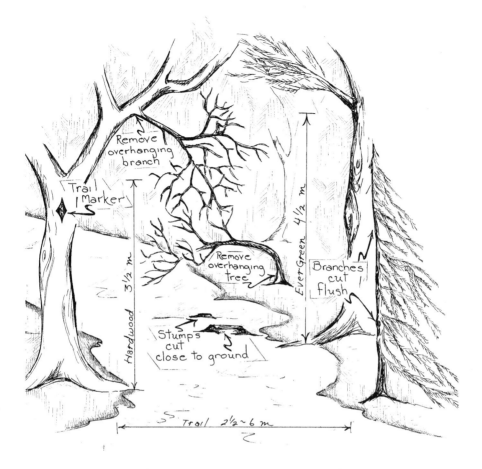

Labels in figure:

Remove overhanging branch

Trail Marker

Hardwood 3½ m

Remove overhanging tree

Evergreen 4½ m

Branches cut flush

Stumps cut close to ground

Trail 2½~6 m

Brush ski trail right of way as shown.

brush on the downhill side of a sloped traverse can also do the same job by collecting and holding snow to create a terrace. Place brush and logs in depressions and around rocks or high roots to provide fill on which snow will collect, making a smoother tread. Be sure that brush used for this does not have limbs that will protrude to create a hazard.

Use log corduroy, hay, or brush to traverse wet or boggy areas that cannot be avoided. Ditching can also be effective, but ditches may present an obstacle requiring a small bridge. Culverts can solve this problem by cross-draining the trail; keep in mind that they generally require a wetlands permit. Culverts can result in large washouts if not installed properly and maintained regularly, and they can freeze and clog. Be certain to get the right size; it can't hurt to go a size larger for good measure. Smooth-bore plastic culverts are more resistant to clogging than corrugated metal and are light enough to drag in the woods easily.

Gradient—Variety and challenge should be objectives for all ski touring trails, so avoid those grinding, sustained uphill or downhill grades and long, flat, boring sections. Over the length of any trail a terrain mix of approximately one-third flat, one-third uphill, and one-third downhill is good.

Grades of 7–8 percent or less are recommended for novice trails. Intermediate trails should have extended grades of no more than 12–15 percent, while expert trails should have long sections with grades no greater than 20–25 percent. A 40 percent grade is generally considered the maximum for even expert skiers. Short sections of higher-than-average grade are acceptable at all three levels of difficulty.

Remember that the steeper the grade, the wider the trail should be to allow skiers to snowplow and herringbone. On corners, widening alone isn't always sufficient. Provide run-outs on corners with steep slopes by clearing the outside of the corner from just before where it begins and continuing well past it. The turning radius of corners should increase as slope increases.

Switchbacks may be necessary in some cases to reduce the grade and shorten the length of the downhill run. Remember again to make those turns wide.

The table on the following page shows the approximate distances a skier will go in attaining speed on slopes of varying degrees of steepness. These estimates should prove useful in field inspections, where it may be necessary to gauge permissible grades in combination with length of run-out and angles of turns.

| Grade | | Maximum Length in Feet |
In Percentages	In Degrees	to Reach 20 MPH
10	6	250–300
12	7	100–125
15	9	80
20	12	60
25	14	40
30	17	30

From New York State Department of Environmental Conservation

Length—Novice trails should generally be three to five miles in length or less. Intermediate trails—possibly a combination of both easy and more difficult trails—can be five to eight miles. Expert trails can be longer. Integrated systems of novice, intermediate, and expert trails provide opportunities for trips of varied length and accommodate the afternoon, evening, and full-day skier.

Stream Crossings and Bridges

Natural stream crossings are cheaper and easier to maintain. For cross-country skiing, natural crossings are best where the stream is slow and not too deep, so it will freeze early in the winter and

Treating wet areas.

remain frozen. Shallow water is safer should a skier break through the ice. Seek gently sloped stream banks that provide an easy crossing.

While there may be sufficient snow cover to ski on a trail, stream crossings, even small ones, may not yet have frozen or may have opened up during a thaw, preventing skiing. Bridges will lengthen the ski season. The same basic construction principles apply to ski trail bridges as to footbridges with one major difference: width. Build ski touring bridges at least eight feet wide and preferably twelve feet wide to hold snow and compensate for crowning. Add a curb of small-diameter logs or 4 x 4 lumber on each edge to retain snow. If grooming equipment is used on the trail, don't forget to build the bridge strong enough to support the added weight.

Ski bridges can be made of native or pressure-treated lumber, though again, native lumber will not last long. Bridges of up to twenty-four feet long can be built using pressure-treated, triple-laminated 2 x 12s (see chapter 8). If you can't truck materials to the site, you may be able to skid them in by snowmobile in the winter.

CROWN + CURB ON X-COUNTRY SKI BRIDGE

Log ski bridge decked with planks for hiking.

Since it is under the snow, the decking of a ski trail bridge does not need to provide good footing as does a footbridge. The decking can be made from small-diameter logs, split logs, or rough planking. Spacing between decking should be 1/2 inch or less to hold snow. Wind blowing up from beneath the bridge can blast snow out of large gaps, leaving hazardous troughs in the snow. Use snow fence and hay to fill in large spaces between pieces of decking. Make decking perpendicular to the direction of skier travel to keep skis from slipping down into the space between. If parallel stringers without decking are used alone, fit them tightly together or "chink" gaps with sticks nailed into place. Place a lumber walkway down the center of a rough-decked bridge to accommodate summer traffic.

Each end of a ski trail bridge should be graded and smooth. Skiers must not be able to catch ski tips on the exposed end of a bridge or its stringers. If more height is needed, add a ramp or fill in the low spot with rocks or logs and brush in corduroy fashion.

Install railings on at least one side of bridges three feet up or higher. Be sure to allow for snow depth when determining the railing height. Do not leave railing ends protruding, especially if skiers will be traveling with speed when crossing. If the approach to a bridge involves a slope that will propel the skier at any speed, avoid railings unless the bridge is very high. A crash into a railing can break skis, poles, and bones. A tumble off one edge of a bridge into snow may be less hazardous.

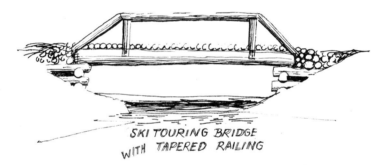

SKI TOURING BRIDGE
WITH TAPERED RAILING

Shovel and pack snow onto the deck after the first snowfall to develop and maintain a better and more complete base. Later in the winter the dark, exposed edges of the decking will warm quickly in the sunlight and snow will begin to melt and recede inward from the edges of the bridge, leaving the track on a high, narrow bank of snow in the middle. The center, after being packed by skis all winter, will be more dense and resistant to melting. To counteract this effect, break the center snow ridge down and scatter it across the decking, or shovel more snow onto the edges. Some maintainers leave a snow shovel hanging on the bridge or a nearby tree for this work.

Where ski trails cross shallow wet or boggy areas, which may freeze late or thaw early, you can place boughs, hay, or log corduroy as an alternative to bridging. For trail drainage, use culverts; water bars tend to create mounds in the trail that thaw out, leaving an open ditch to traverse on the uphill side.

Avoid crossings of bogs, ponds, and lakes; they can be dangerous when the ice is thin. Provide alternate routes if water crossings are part of a trail.

Standard diamond-shaped ski trail marker.

Trail Signing and Marking

Post the difficulty rating of a trail and information on distances at all trailheads and junctions and on maps of the area. If you can afford it, provide a large map of the entire area and all the trails at a main trailhead. Information on trail conditions, recommended wax of the day, and trail closures should be made available at a central location.

The standard difficulty markers used by most ski touring organizations are most often printed on heavy plastic. They have been adopted by the U.S. Forest Service, U.S. Ski Association, and Cross Country Ski Areas Association. A red exclamation point on a yellow plastic triangle is used to mark the beginning of a steep descent or a sharp corner.

Four-inch azure blue, plastic diamonds are the standard used to mark most ski trails. All plastic signs and markers can be purchased through the Cross Country Ski Areas Association (CCSAA), 259 Bolton Road, Winchester, NH 03470 (phone: 603-239-4341; fax: 603-239-6387; and e-mail: ccsaa@xcski.org). CCSAA also publishes extensive design and operations manuals.

Place signs and markers approximately five feet above the highest level of snow cover. When nailing them to trees, use aluminum nails, and leave the heads sticking out about one inch to allow for tree growth. If you do not, the tree will grow outward over the nail, causing the sign or marker to pucker up. Aluminum nails will not damage sawmill or pulp-mill equipment, should the tree eventually be logged. Mark treeless areas or areas with extremely deep snow by using poles set in the snow.

Mapping

Any map for a ski touring trail or system should be easy to read, accurate, and should include references to the difficulty rating of each trail. Trails and junctions can be numbered or lettered in the field and on the map for easy reference by skiers. Maps should also include phone numbers for local emergency services.

Facilities

Consider providing warming huts, overnight shelter, and strategically placed first-aid caches on longer trails in remote or rough areas.

CHAPTER TEN
Tools: Use and Care

The types of tools used in trail maintenance will vary depending on the type of work. One should always have the right tools for the job. The purpose of this chapter is to acquaint the trail maintainer with various types of tools and equipment and to outline their proper use, care, and applicable safety procedures.

In addition to describing hand tools, this chapter will discuss some basic power tools. However, information provided on their use is limited. Professional users and manufacturers can supply a great deal more information on selecting and safely operating power equipment.

Experience has taught that only top-quality tools should be purchased. Using bargain tools will usually only result in headaches for trail workers and could possibly compromise their safety.

Cutting Tools

Cutting tools are one of the most important type used in trail work. They are used to clear trails of trees and brush during their initial development, and annually thereafter. Also, cutting tools are used to build all sorts of wooden trail structures.

Cutting tools are the most difficult and elaborate tools in terms of the maintenance they require; in addition, high-quality tools may be hard to find. Many stores carry simple tools such as axes, saws, and pruners; however, contemporary tools are often drop-forged, made of poor-quality steel, shoddily constructed, and meant only for light use by homeowners. The best-quality hand tools are hand-forged antique tools found at flea markets and antique stores. A little elbow grease will dispose of a light patina of rust to reveal a tool superior to any commercially available today.

Tools in this category include axes, saws, pruners, brush cutters, and specialized tools such as brush or bush hooks and safety axes.

The Ax

The ax is undoubtedly one of man's oldest tools. It has played a tremendously important role throughout history. It was in America that the ax reached its highest form; nowhere else in the world has it been used so much, undergone so many changes, and seen so many adaptations to different uses. Unfortunately, today the ax is losing its importance and popularity. Because of this it is very difficult to find a good ax made with high-quality steel.

The ax continues to be an important tool in trail work. On the AMC trail crew it is the primary tool used to cut logs for trail reconstruction and remove winter blowdowns.

If used correctly and maintained properly, the ax can be just as effective, efficient, and safe as the crosscut saw or even (in the case of long-distance backcountry trail work) the chain saw. It is lighter than the chain saw and does not require as many accessories. In addition to being a very practical tool for trail work, it is also a very aesthetic tool which, because of its ancient roots, has great appeal for many trail workers. Aside from replacing the handle every couple of years, maintaining an ax is an expense-free proposition, unlike the continued cost of operating a chain saw.

The two basic kinds of axes are the single bit and the double bit.

Both can be used for removing blowdowns, felling trees, limbing, cutting notches and water bars, and topping bridges.

The single bit is the more familiar of the two types. The double bit was more popular in the past, when axmen needed to have two

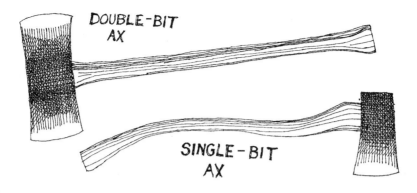

DOUBLE-BIT AX

SINGLE-BIT AX

blades, one that was kept extremely sharp for felling, limbing, and notching and the other for chopping close to the ground or in situations that would otherwise dull the good edge. Some feel that the double bit is better balanced, the cutting edge being balanced by the duller edge at the other end of the blade.

For safety reasons a single bit is most popular today. The flat head of the single-bit ax can also be helpful for occasionally pounding stakes or spikes. However, care should be used in this situation, because the ax head can quite easily be beaten out of shape and the eye become too wide for the wooden handle. It is best to use a sledgehammer for operations that require heavy pounding.

The ax is a very personal tool. The type of ax as well as its weight and the style of the head is usually a matter of taste on the part of the ax owner. However, the job that the ax is going to be used for is also an important criterion. Single-bit axes are the easiest to find, and therefore will probably be the best choice for most people.

The size of the ax is one personal aspect of choosing a good tool. Normally, chopping work is done with a 3- to 3 1/2-pound ax head. Smaller people may prefer a lighter axe. Bigger people might want a 4- or even 4 1/2-pound axe; however, they should probably try one out before selecting this larger size. In addition to the weight of the head, the length of the handle is an important consideration. Shorter people (under 5'8") want a smaller ax handle (28–30 inches), whereas taller people want a longer one (32–36 inches). If the ax is going to be used for clearing small brush and working in cramped quarters, then a smaller handle is more appropriate.

A good-quality ax is made of two different kinds of steel. Mild steel, which is softer and therefore more resistant to impact, makes up the eye or the body of the axe. The edge of the ax is made of a harder carbon steel that is forged to the body; it will take and hold a sharp edge. Most axes that are available today are drop-forged and made of one kind of steel. Because of this they may be hard and brittle, making it difficult to maintain a good edge. They may also be somewhat more prone to metal fatigue. Some of these drop-forged axes have broken when they have been used on frozen or hard wood. When shopping for an ax look for a seam and hammer marks between the eye and the edge of the axe; this indicates that it is made of two different kinds of steel. An ax head that is painted or otherwise obscured, especially in the vicinity of the edge, is probably drop-forged. A good place to look for a high-quality two-steel ax is at an antique store. The older axes found in such circumstances are often handmade and of generally higher quality than modern mass-produced axes.

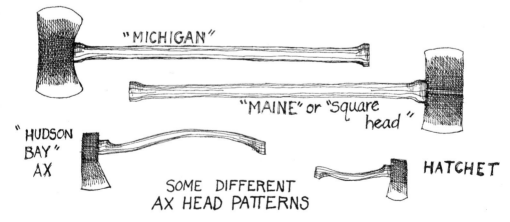

"MICHIGAN"

"MAINE" or "Square head"

"HUDSON BAY" AX

HATCHET

SOME DIFFERENT AX HEAD PATTERNS

USE A LOW-SPEED
WHEEL AND KEEP
IT **WET**
ALSO NOTE ANGLE
OF AX TO
WHEEL

In addition to axes for cutting clean timber, most crews also have a "root ax," usually a lower-quality single bit maintained with a fairly blunt edge. Root axes are indispensable for cutting not just roots but any wood close to the ground where a good ax would surely be damaged.

Sharpening an Ax

All cutting tools, including axes, are actually safest when kept sharp. This allows the ax to more easily penetrate the wood, reducing fatigue and hazardous glancing blows. Sharp tools are obviously more efficient too.

Sharpening an ax well can be tedious; however, it is a fairly straightforward process, requiring only time, practice, and a few simple implements. The most critical aspect of the ax edge is the *bevel*, which is the shape of the edge itself.

In the illustration, bevel A usually develops in an older ax that has been improperly maintained. Sharpening has obviously been concentrated on the edge, which in turn has rounded out the steel into a fairly blunt profile. Bevel B is the proper bevel. The ax is thin enough so that it penetrates deeply into wood but not too thin, as in bevel C. A thin bevel is apt to stick in the wood without knock-

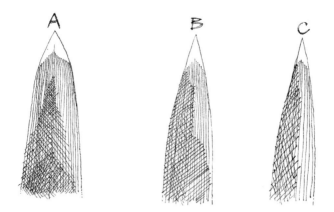

A   B   C

ing the chips loose, and makes the edge fragile and prone to break-ing. To work a bevel down and get it into shape, as in B, work the steel down with either a good manual stone wheel or a mill bastard file.

When using a wheel, always keep its surface wet to carry away any grit that could clog it up, and to prevent friction and overheating of the ax head. Never use an electric grinding wheel to sharpen an ax, as it can overheat and destroy the temper of the steel.

A mill bastard file works well for sharpen-ing axes; it is also inexpen-sive and can be brought into the work site. Always sharpen into the blade; oth-erwise, the edge will develop a small piece of wirelike metal that will break off with use. By sharp-ening into the blade, little or no burr will form. Use extreme care when sharpening with a file, because the hand is pushing in the direc-tion of the blade. A file can be fitted with a handle and hand guard. Cut a four-inch square of leather or old fire hose; cut a hole through the center; slip it over the tang of the file and put the handle on. Wear a good pair of heavy leather gloves when working.

FILE DIAGONALLY INTO EDGE

WATCH YOUR FINGERS

Work the bevel down until it looks thin enough to cut properly (bevel B) and has a consistently even and slightly curved shape. Once the proper bevel is attained, take a round hand stone and hone the edge smooth. Use water or a light oil on hand stones. If a very keen edge is desired, a finer stone such as an Arkansas hand stone can be used. This final part of the process can produce an edge that is fine enough to shave a hair, although many people achieve an excellent edge with just a file. A sharpening stone may be preferable

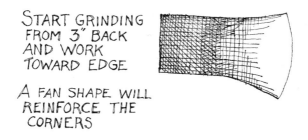

START GRINDING FROM 3" BACK AND WORK TOWARD EDGE

A FAN SHAPE WILL REINFORCE THE CORNERS

for maintaining a good edge, since frequent filing rapidly wears down the blade.

Again, an ax should be kept as sharp as possible at all times. Maintaining a keen edge is well worth the effort.

Rehandling an Ax

Handles require eventual replacement. Over time they will warp, crack, break, or shrink. The ax head may loosen, so you may need to replace the handle.

The first step is removal of the old handle. The easiest and fastest way to do this is to saw the handle off close to the ax head. Then place the head in a vise or on wooden blocks and drill out as much wood as you can from the eye of the ax with an electric or hand-operated drill. By boring out these holes, the pressure of the wood within the ax head is relieved so that the wood can be pounded out with a hammer and a blunt metal object.

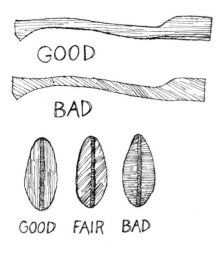

GOOD

BAD

GOOD   FAIR   BAD

PAY CLOSE ATTENTION TO
THE END GRAIN— A TIGHT
GRAIN PARALLEL TO THE
WEDGE IS BEST

Choose a new handle with a length that will fit the ax. When purchasing a new handle look closely at the grain of the wood. It should be fairly straight, close together, and parallel with the axis of the handle and the ax head. If not, it is probably weak and prone to breaking. Avoid knots and other defects at all costs.

Hickory is the best wood for handles because it has a lot of spring and strength. Avoid handles that are painted, since painting often conceals faults in the wood.

The next step involves fitting the handle into the eye. The handle needs to be shaped to closely match the eye of the ax in order to fit tightly. Use a draw knife, wood rasp, or spoke shave to shape the top of the handle down to the size of the eye. Remove wood cautiously, a little at a time, so that you do not make the handle too thin. Once you can get the handle to slide into one-third of the eye, test the fit by pounding the handle into the head. Hold the handle, ax head down, and drive the handle down into the eye by pounding the base of the handle with a wooden or leather mallet or old mattock handle. You can also drive the ax head down onto the handle by setting the head onto the handle and pounding the base of the handle straight down onto a block of wood on the floor or a stump. Be careful the head doesn't spring off the handle. See how it fits and where you need to take off more wood. Knock the head off the handle with a block of wood or mattock handle and shave off more wood where needed. Try the fit again. You'll probably need to test the fit and fine-tune the handle a few times until you achieve the desired fit.

Once you get a good fit, soundly pound the handle home so the ax head wedges tightly on the handle at its proper place. An inch or so of the top of the handle should be sticking out past the top of the ax head; saw off this excess wood flush with the ax head.

Next, drive a hardwood wedge into the cut handle slot, now inside the eye of the ax head. Cut off any excess wedge when

DRIVE HANDLE INTO HEAD WITH A WOODEN OR LEATHER MALLET

it will go no deeper. Wooden wedges, usually supplied with a new handle, compress as they are driven in and expand inside the head, wedging it on tightly. The wedge may split as you drive it in; that's fine, as some pieces will go deeper and fill wider gaps. One or two small steel wedges can be driven in perpendicular to the wooden one for more security.

Care of the Handle

New handles come with either a paint or a hard varnish finish that can cause blistered hands. Sand off the finish and rub in a coat of boiled linseed oil with a rag; this keeps the handle flexible and protects it from rot and drying, which can lead to cracking and shrinking. A periodic coating of boiled linseed oil will help prevent these problems and give the handle a smooth finish.

FEED YOUR AX

PUT LINSEED OIL IN THE HOLES DRILLED IN THE HANDLE — ADD S LIFE!

To help extend the life of a handle, linseed oil can be periodically placed in one or two holes drilled in the end of the handle. The holes should be about 1/4 inch in diameter and 1/2 inch deep. At the end of the work trip, place several drops of linseed oil in the holes and set the ax handle upright to soak overnight. The natural capillary action of the wood will draw the oil into the grain.

If a handle shrinks and loosens within the head of the ax, a temporary solution is to soak the ax head in a bucket of water overnight. This causes the wood to swell and tighten within the head. Remember, this is only a temporary solution. Oil the ax head before immersion to retard rust. Replacing or adding a wedge may help, but the handle should eventually be replaced.

Do not store an ax for a long period of time by leaning it in a corner, as the handle will develop a bend. Hang it up instead.

Ax Sheaths

All axes should be sheathed when being transported or stored to protect both the edge of the ax and people. Many kinds of sheaths can be purchased or made. The most common ones are leather sheaths with snaps or straps.

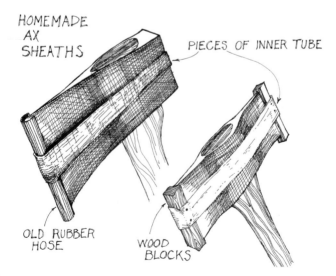

HOMEMADE AX SHEATHS

PIECES OF INNER TUBE

OLD RUBBER HOSE

WOOD BLOCKS

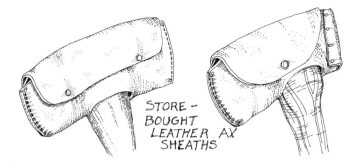

STORE-
BOUGHT
LEATHER AX
SHEATHS

Simple sheaths can be made using rubber from an old garden hose. The hose is cut to the width of the blade and slit along its length. The hose is held against the edge of the ax with a piece of rubber inner tube. Another type of sheath can be made by hollowing a block of wood to fit over the edge of the ax. Wood is less prone to slip off the blade and is stronger than rubber hose. Staple or screw the inner tube to the wood sheath to hold it in place against the ax.

Pulaski

This tool, a single-bit ax with a small grub-hoe blade designed for fighting fires, is somewhat popular. It can be used for sidehill grubbing, cutting roots, removing blowdowns, cleaning drainages, and other trail maintenance.

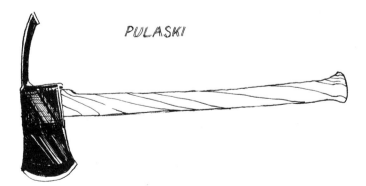

PULASKI

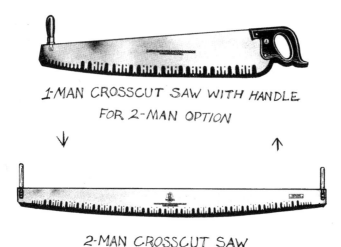

1-MAN CROSSCUT SAW WITH HANDLE
FOR 2-MAN OPTION

2-MAN CROSSCUT SAW

Crosscut Saws

There are two types of crosscut saws. The one-person crosscut, generally 3 to 4 1/2 feet in length, is designed to be used by one person on small timber. It can be converted into a two-person saw if desired by attaching a supplementary handle at the end of the blade. The two-person crosscut, usually 5 to 8 feet in length, is designed for cutting larger-diameter timber. There are two basic two-person saw patterns. The *felling saw*, for cutting down trees, has a concave back and is relatively lightweight and flexible. The *bucking saw*, for cutting up felled trees, has a flat back and is heavier and stiffer for faster vertical cutting.

Three common tooth patterns are available, each designed for a specific type of wood. The perforated lance-tooth style is best for cutting softwoods. The champion-tooth style is for cutting hard-

PERFORATED LANCE TOOTH

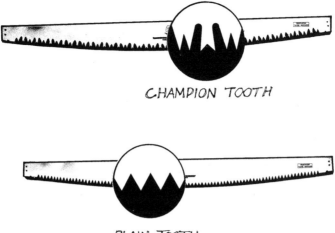

CHAMPION TOOTH

PLAIN TOOTH

woods or frozen timber, and is most often used with one-person-saws. The plain-tooth style is designed for cutting dead, dry wood.

The teeth of a plain-tooth saw both cut the wood and remove the shavings. On perforated lance and champion-tooth saws the cutting teeth sever the wood fibers on each side of the cut. The raker teeth, cutting like a plane bit, peel the cut fibers and collect them in the gullets between the cutting teeth and raker teeth and carry them out of the cut. A properly sharpened crosscut saw cuts deep and makes thick shavings.

As few people know how to properly maintain a crosscut saw, they are not often used today. The ax, chain saw, and bow saw are more commonly used. Like the ax, the crosscut has somewhat become a tool of the past with the introduction of the chain saw.

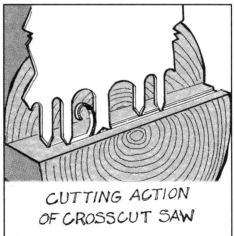

CUTTING ACTION
OF CROSSCUT SAW

Crosscuts do, however, have some advantages over the ax and even the chain saw that make them a good choice for large cutting projects. They are inexpensive, lightweight, nonpolluting (of noise and fumes), safer than an ax, and relatively easy to use. They are often the tool of choice for working in wilderness areas where motorized equipment is not allowed. They can be just as effective as a chain saw, especially when the tool must be carried long distances. Sometimes, however, finding someone to properly sharpen a crosscut can be difficult. Small, relatively inexpensive sharpening kits can be obtained, as well as excellent instructions for performing your own crosscut maintenance.

There are a few use and safety tips to keep in mind. When felling timber you should use the same basic technique as outlined for felling with a chain saw or ax (see chapter 6). To keep your crosscut from binding, carry a small container of kerosene or diesel fuel and lightly coat the blade with it. For transporting a crosscut, a sheath can be made of a section of old fire hose, slit along its length and tied or strapped over the teeth. You can also use two strips of plywood held together over the blade with three or four bolts.

Bow Saws and Pruning Saws

Bow saws, sometimes known as pulpwood saws, and the smaller, curved-blade pruning saws come in a wide variety of sizes and shapes. Bow saws cut on both a pulling and pushing stroke; pruning saws cut on a pull stroke only. The choice of saw depends on the size and amount of wood to be cut. Some older bow saws have wooden frames: today, most have painted or chrome-plated steel or aluminum frames and blades ranging in length from 24 to 36 inches. Pruning-saw blades range from 10 to 24 inches in length; some conveniently fold up like a jackknife.

Larger bow saws can be used for cutting moderate-size timber and for removing blowdowns.

Smaller bow saws and pruning saws are good for sawing small-diameter timber and clearing trail where saplings or limbs are too large for clippers. They also won't leave undesirable pointed stumps, as sometimes happens when using an ax or brush hook. There are some collapsible bow saws which are handy for occasional use but are generally too lightweight for continuous, heavy-duty use.

A good small bow saw.

Various types of long-handled pole pruning saws are useful for cutting high limbs when clearing ski touring trails.

When using these saws, be sure that all moving parts such as nuts and bolts are secure and that bow saw blades are at the right tension. Blades that are too loose or too tight can break or get pinched in the wood. Trail experience favors saws with the fewest number of movable parts (such as wing nuts), which may get lost. Most bow saws and pruning saws have blades that are replaced rather than sharpened. Bring spare blades and parts when working in the field so that minor repairs can be made.

When transporting or storing saws, some type of sheath should be used to protect the worker as well as the blade. Wood, leather, or pieces of garden hose can be used. Many bow saws come with hard plastic sheaths. All unpainted metal parts should be kept lightly oiled to prevent rust.

POLE SAW

Lopping Shears, Pole Clippers, and Hand Pruners

Long-handled clippers, pruners, or lopping shears come in a variety of styles. Handles are made of wood, steel, or aluminum. Cutting heads are either the sliding-blade-and-hook type or the anvil type. Some have simple pivot actions, while others have compound or gear-driven actions for increased cutting power. Most cut between 1- and 1 3/4-inch limbs.

For specialized work such as clearing ski touring trails, a variety of pole clippers are manufactured for professional tree-trimming work. These are suitable for clipping high limbs up to 1 or 1 1/2

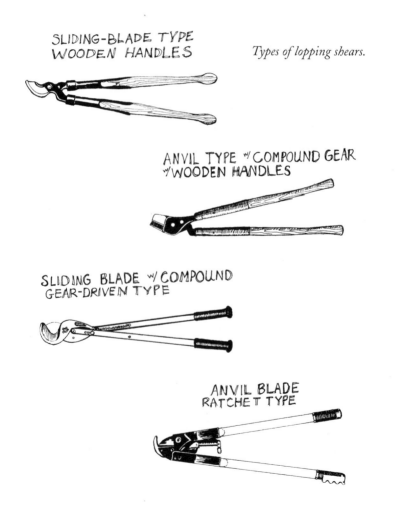

SLIDING-BLADE TYPE
WOODEN HANDLES

Types of lopping shears.

ANVIL TYPE w/ COMPOUND GEAR
w/ WOODEN HANDLES

SLIDING BLADE w/ COMPOUND
GEAR-DRIVEN TYPE

ANVIL BLADE
RATCHET TYPE

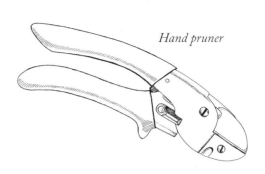

Hand pruner

Pole pruner

inches in diameter. Generally a 6- to 8-foot handle is sufficient for ski touring trail work. Longer handles can be obtained.

Small hand pruners can sometimes be quite handy for occasional light pruning. These also come in a wide variety of styles.

Since clippers or lopping shears are one of the primary tools of the trail maintainer, it is important to purchase high-quality ones. Look for quality brand-name shears that are built for rugged, professional use and are simple to maintain and repair.

Clippers should be kept sharp, with all metal parts lightly oiled. A flat file or hand stone works well for sharpening the blade. For sliding-blade pruners, which work like scissors, sharpen only the outside, beveled edge of the cutting blade.

The anvil-type pruners are sharpened on both sides of the cutting blade with a stone, like a pocketknife. Care must be taken to sharpen such blades evenly along their length. The soft metal anvils

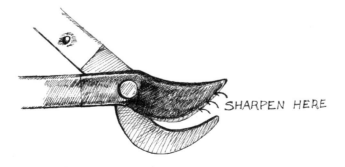

SHARPEN HERE

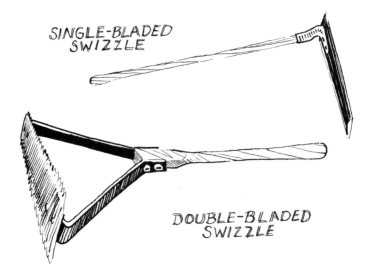

SINGLE-BLADED
SWIZZLE

DOUBLE-BLADED
SWIZZLE

should be adjusted to meet the cutting blade evenly when the pruner is closed.

The Swizzle Stick

This important and versatile tool was developed for clearing brush and low growth along hiking tails. Similar tools are commercially available; however, they generally lack the strength and durability of the homemade variety. Some have straight edges, while others have serrated blades.

A swizzle stick is used in a swinging motion, as with a golf club. One with a double-edged blade enables the worker to cut on the backswing as well. The swizzle should always be swung firmly, with both hands on the handle to fully control the swing. A rock or stump may accidentally deflect the tool; therefore, always wear heavy boots when using this tool. Also, maintain a good distance from other trail workers.

Sharpen a swizzle stick in a similar way as an ax with a bastard file and stone.

A blade sheath should be used when carrying and storing the swizzle. A strip of heavy canvas or old fire hose wrapped around the blade and held in place by inner-tube rubber shaped in a figure-

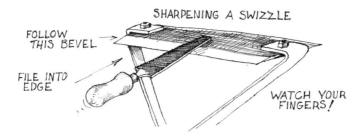

SHARPENING A SWIZZLE

FOLLOW THIS BEVEL

FILE INTO EDGE

WATCH YOUR FINGERS!

eight works well. Adhesive tape can be used in a pinch. A wooden or leather sheath can also be made.

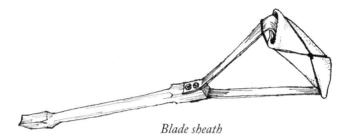

Blade sheath

Constructing a Swizzle Stick

Use hardwood, such as ash or hickory, for the handle. Cut it to size and round the upper part with a lathe or by hand, leaving a knob on the end for a secure grip. In an emergency, a sledgehammer handle will do. The steel frame can be bent with the help of a torch or forge. The blade is the most difficult part, requiring the help of a machinist or blacksmith to fashion a blade of tempered steel needed to hold a good cutting edge.

Use hardened bolts with flat washers for strength. To keep bolts from loosening use lock washers under the nuts. Also, you can peen over the ends of the bolts or use the commercial compound Locktite.

Customize your swizzle stick by lengthening or shortening the handle. Some maintainers wrap black electrician's tape around the handle, sometimes with a thin piece of foam or ensolite, to cushion the handle slightly.

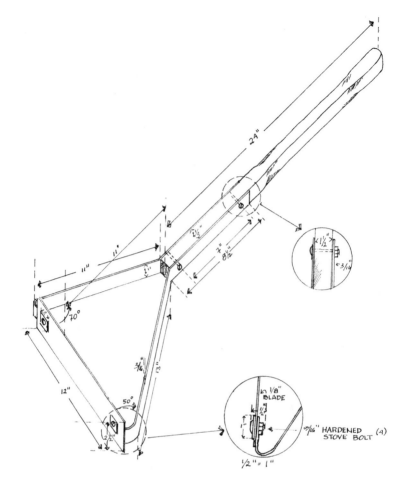

24"

1 1/2"
3/4"

11"
11"
1 1/8"
1"
8 1/2"
70°

1/8"
BLADE
3/16"
13"
12"
50°
2"
1"
1/2" = 1"

3/16" HARDENED (4)
STOVE BOLT

Safety Ax, Brush Hook, and Machete

These can be handy, although somewhat more hazardous, supplements to the more classic tools used for trail clearing. They require care, sheathing, and sharpening similar to that described for the ax.

The safety ax, as the name implies, is a good choice for most trail workers, because the blade is less exposed than that of a brush hook or machete. If the blade is damaged, it can be replaced. Safety axes are particularly effective on young, springy hardwood growth.

The bush or brush hook is another type of tool available for clearing brush.

The best machete for trail clearing is probably the woodsmen's pal. It has some features, such as a cutting hook, that are unavailable

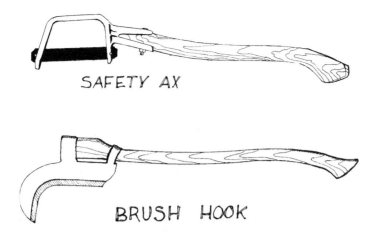

SAFETY AX

BRUSH HOOK

on a conventional machete. It is also shorter than the conventional ones, which allows a shorter, more controlled swing.

As with the swizzle stick, all of these tools should be used with care. A good grip at all times, plenty of space between workers, and looking and concentrating before swinging will prevent accidents and damage to the tools.

Because these tools can be hazardous and often leave a sharply pointed stub when limbing or brushing, most trail workers prefer hand saws or clippers for limbing and other brushing which leave a cleaner, smoother cut and are much safer to use.

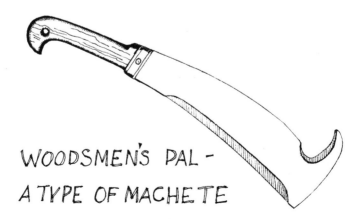

WOODSMEN'S PAL -
A TYPE OF MACHETE

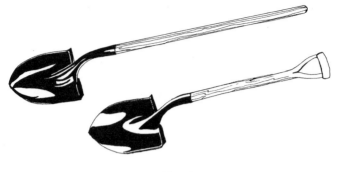

Shovels

Digging Tools

Virtually all trail reconstruction and maintenance activities require that workers move soil and rock to build steps, water bars, drainage ditches, bridges, and similar projects. Digging tools for accomplishing these tasks include the shovel, mattock, hoe, and rock bar.

Shovel

The commonly used round-point shovel comes with either a long handle or D handle.

The shorter D handle shovel is more appropriate in congested situations. Some also find lifting with this type of shovel to be easier, since the load is closer to the body. Others favor the long-handle shovel, because it offers a longer reach and usually requires less bending. Do not pry heavily with the shovel or the handle will break. A mattock or rock bar should be used if large rocks impede digging. Some maintainers slightly sharpen the shovel's edge to facilitate cutting roots.

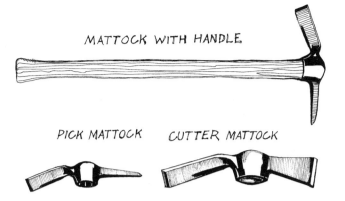

MATTOCK WITH HANDLE

PICK MATTOCK   CUTTER MATTOCK

Mattock

In the White Mountains, with their abundance of rocks and roots, the mattock has become the most important, and favorite, trail tread tool for digging, grubbing, and prying. The mattock is a heavy, hard-working tool that is not easily broken. The mattock is capable of chopping through roots, loosening compacted soils, and prying out and even breaking rock. It is indispensable for levering rocks into position for steps, cribbing, and water bars.

Two types of mattocks are available, both of which have an adze or a blade set at right angles to the handle for grubbing. They differ by having either a pick or a cutter blade at the other end.

The pick mattock is more popular with AMC crews because it is much more effective for prying rock. The cutter mattock may be more effective in areas with deeper soils and more roots than rocks.

Care consists of periodic slight sharpening in order to maintain a rudimentary edge capable of effective digging and root cutting.

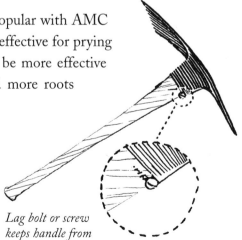

Lag bolt or screw keeps handle from working loose.

An electric grinding wheel, carefully used to avoid overheating the edge, reduces labor time when sharpening. Handles should get a periodic coating of boiled linseed oil; damaged handles should be replaced.

To keep handles from working loose prematurely, screw a 3/16" x 1" lag bolt into the handle up against the mattock head. Drill a pilot hole first. Do not place it in the side of the handle, as this may cause it to split. This should be done to grub and adze hoes also.

Grub Hoes and Adze Hoes

Hoes of various styles are used in trail construction and maintenance. They are particularly useful for duffing new trail, sidehill grubbing, and building and cleaning drainages.

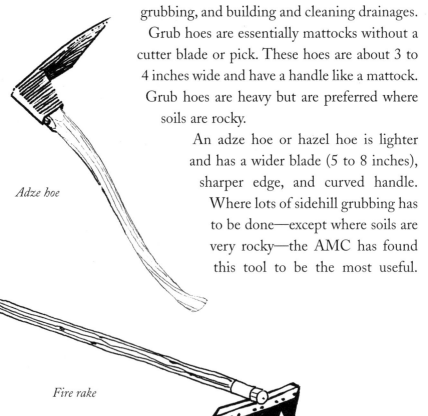

Grub hoes are essentially mattocks without a cutter blade or pick. These hoes are about 3 to 4 inches wide and have a handle like a mattock. Grub hoes are heavy but are preferred where soils are rocky.

An adze hoe or hazel hoe is lighter and has a wider blade (5 to 8 inches), sharper edge, and curved handle. Where lots of sidehill grubbing has to be done—except where soils are very rocky—the AMC has found this tool to be the most useful.

Adze hoe

Fire rake

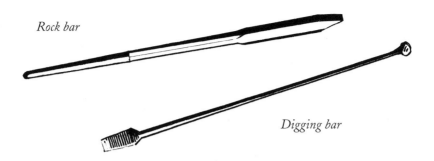

Rock bar

Digging bar

The wider blade moves more soil, the sharper edge cuts roots well, and the curved handle facilitates use.

Fire Rakes

Fire rakes are very useful for duffing new trail and are also used to clean drainages primarily clogged with leaves and loose soil.

Pick

A pick is rarely necessary in trail work, its function being adequately served by the pick mattock. However, for loosening compacted earth or chipping rock, picks may be appropriate.

Rock Bar

Sixteen- to eighteen-pound hardened-steel rock bars, about 4 1/2 feet long with a beveled tip, are the best choice. Lighter ones are apt to bend; shorter ones provide less leverage. This tool is essential for moving large and small rocks. The rock bar's length and the fulcruming ability of its chisel-shaped tip provide the mechanical advantage needed to move great weights.

A long digging bar is used for loosening compacted or rocky soil. It has a small blade at one end. These bars can be used to move smaller rocks, but they don't have the stiffness of a rock bar needed to lever large rocks.

Hoisting Tools

Ratchet Winches

A ratchet winch is often used for moving large rocks or logs. Most are available with varying pull capacities, anywhere from one to four tons. They utilize a cable on a spool and can be used as a single or double cable.

Griphoist

See chapter 6 for more on the griphoist.

Measuring Tools

Ratchet winch

Various tools for measuring distances may be required during lay-out, reconstruction, and maintenance of trails. *Levels, measuring tapes,* and *clinometers* are used for laying out a trail or campsite, or for constructing stream bridges and ladders.

Measuring wheels are used to measure trail distances for guide-book descriptions. They are also used for locating and indexing trail features and creating work logs to guide work crews. The AMC has had the best luck with an inexpensive, rugged, all-steel measuring

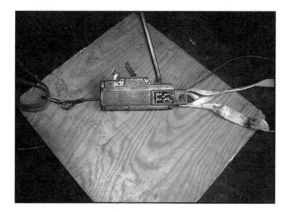

Griphoist shown with anchor and rock sling.

wheel with an internal cable and counter mecha-
nism on the handle made by Cedarholm. Those
with external counters, which sometimes get caught on brush, or bicy-
cle-like wheels, which can get bent
easily, have not worked as well.
Some enterprising maintainers
have made their own measuring
tools using a bicycle mileage
meter and wheel.

*Measuring
wheel*

Power Tools

Though the bulk of trail work involves the
use of hand tools, there are occasions where concentrations of heavy
cutting or specialized work make power tools more efficient.
Information on the chain saw, motorized brush cutter, and jackhammer are included here. Only a broad description of each tool
and its specifications is given; get specific information from manufacturers on the use and care of these implements.

Chain Saws

This cursory overview is provided to help people select and purchase saws. The manufacturers supply extensive information that
the careful shopper should read. The opinions of friends and fellow
maintainers are also obvious, and dependable, sources of good information on the comparative value of different saws. It may also be
beneficial to talk to either a professional tree-trimming outfit or a
logging operator working in the purchaser's local area. The types of
saws they use and their recommendations on dealerships may be
helpful.

The chain saw comes in a variety of makes, sizes, and types—
each suited to a particular job. Each of the major manufacturers of

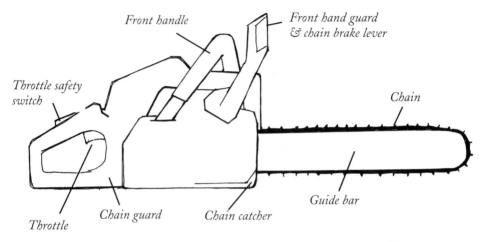

Front handle

Front hand guard
& chain brake lever

Throttle safety
switch

Chain

Chain guard

Chain catcher

Guide bar

Throttle

Chainsaw

chain saws carries a full line of equipment that graduates in size and power from small, light-duty saws to the large machines used by the pulp and paper industry.

Choosing a make, model, and options is a matter of personal taste, like choosing an automobile. First figure out what kind of work you'll be doing with the saw and then find a local dealer who can help you make the appropriate purchase. Make sure the saw has the best safety features and is easy to operate and maintain in the field. Having a good dealer who provides prompt and efficient service and safe operating instructions is equally important. Avoid chain saws sold by the large department store outlets.

Smaller saws are naturally the most popular saws for trail work because of their light weight. Larger, more powerful saws are more appropriate for heavy cutting, such as cleaning up a trail damaged by a major storm or timber harvesting. These situations are rare for most maintainers, however.

Safe Chain Saw Operation

Safe chain saw operating techniques should be constantly stressed to all users. The chain operates at a fast cutting speed and the slightest slip or miscalculation can cause serious injury.

Personal protective equipment critical for the safe operation of chain saws includes helmets, eye protection, face protection, and ear protection. Chain saw operators must always wear chaps to protect their legs from the fast running chain. Additionally, leather gloves should be worn, as well as heavy boots with nonslip soles, preferably equipped with steel toe shields. Well-fitting, long-sleeved shirts and long pants are also warranted.

CHECKLIST FOR THE SAFE AND EFFICIENT OPERATION OF YOUR CHAIN SAW

▶ READ YOUR OWNER'S MANUAL AND ALL SUPPLEMENTS thoroughly before operating your saw.

▶ USE THE PERSONAL PROTECTIVE EQUIPMENT LISTED ABOVE.

▶ DON'T USE ANY OTHER FUEL than that recommended in your owner's manual.

▶ REFUEL IN A SAFE PLACE. Don't spill fuel or start the saw where you fuel it. Do not refuel a hot saw; allow it to cool off. Be certain the saw has dried thoroughly before starting, if fuel has spilled on the unit.

▶ DON'T SMOKE while fueling or operating the saw.

▶ START YOUR SAW WITHOUT HELP. Don't start a saw on your leg or knee. Never operate a chain saw when you are fatigued.

▶ KEEP ALL PARTS of your body and clothing away from the saw chain when starting or running the engine. Before you start the engine, make sure the saw chain is not in contact with anything.

Continued on next page

- ▶ BEWARE OF KICKBACK! Hold saw firmly with both hands when engine is running; use a firm grip with thumbs and fingers encircling the chain saw handles and watch carefully what you cut. Kickback (saw jumps or jerks up or backward) can be caused by:

  - Striking limbs or other objects accidentally with the tip of the saw while the chain is moving.

  - Striking metal, cement, or other hard material near the wood, or buried in the wood.

  - Running engine slowly at start of or during cut.

  - Dull or loose chain.

  - Cutting above shoulder height.

  - Inattention in holding or guiding saw while cutting.

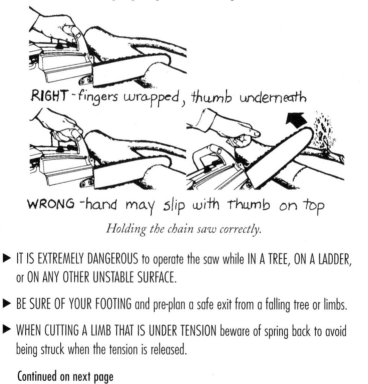

RIGHT - fingers wrapped, thumb underneath

WRONG - hand may slip with thumb on top

Holding the chain saw correctly.

- ▶ IT IS EXTREMELY DANGEROUS to operate the saw while IN A TREE, ON A LADDER, or ON ANY OTHER UNSTABLE SURFACE.

- ▶ BE SURE OF YOUR FOOTING and pre-plan a safe exit from a falling tree or limbs.

- ▶ WHEN CUTTING A LIMB THAT IS UNDER TENSION beware of spring back to avoid being struck when the tension is released.

Continued on next page

- ▶ USE EXTREME CAUTION when cutting small brush and saplings because slender material may catch the saw chain and be whipped toward you or pull you off balance.

- ▶ VIBRATION—Avoid prolonged operation of your chain saw and rest periodically. Stop using the saw if your hand or arm starts to have a loss of feeling, swells, or becomes difficult to move.

- ▶ EXHAUST FUMES—Do not operate your chain saw in confined or poorly ventilated areas.

- ▶ OBSERVE ALL LOCAL FIRE-PREVENTION REGULATIONS—It is recommended that you keep a fire extinguisher and shovel close at hand whenever you cut in areas where dry grass, leaves, or other flammable materials are present.

- ▶ TURN OFF YOUR SAW WHEN MOVING BETWEEN CUTS and before setting it down. Always carry the chain saw with the engine stopped, the guide bar and saw chain in the rear, and the muffler away from your body.

- ▶ USE WEDGES TO HELP CONTROL FELLING and prevent binding the bar and chain in the cut.

- ▶ DON'T TOUCH or try to stop a moving chain with your hand.

- ▶ KEEP THE CHAIN SHARP and snug on the guide bar.

- ▶ DON'T ALLOW DIRT, FUEL, OR SAWDUST to build up on the engine or outside of the saw.

- ▶ KEEP ALL SCREWS AND FASTENERS TIGHT. Never operate a chain saw that is damaged, improperly adjusted, or not completely and securely assembled. Be sure that the saw chain stops moving when the throttle-control trigger is released. Keep the handles dry, clean, and free of oil or fuel mixture.

Gas–Powered Brush Cutters

Much like a heavy-duty weed whacker with a metal blade for cutting wood, these power tools are useful for extensive trail clearing through young, heavy growth. Most clearing can be done by hand

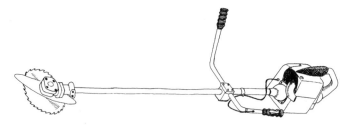

Gas-powered brush cutter

and few maintainers have the need to invest in this specialized piece of equipment. If one is used, the operator should be experienced and maintain a safe working distance from others.

Jackhammers and Rock Drills

These tools are self-contained and powered by a single-cylinder, two-cycle gasoline engine. They provide power to chisel away or shape rock and drill holes for splitting rock and anchoring pins. They can be packed into remote locations by two crew members, one to carry the drill, the other to carry fuel and all accessories.

Other Tools

Bark spuds or *peelers* can greatly facilitate peeling logs for trail construction. Before the modern, automated debarkers used at sawmills and paper mills were invented, all bark removal was done by hand using these simple but effective tools.

Bark spud

Splitting wedges or *wood chopper's wedges*, most commonly used to split firewood, are also used to split logs for bridges. Generally a 4- to 5-pound wedge, 8 to 10 inches long and 2 1/2 to 3 inches wide, is best.

Splitting wedge

Timber carriers can sometimes be used to carry large logs for water bars, bog bridges, and stream bridges, as well as for shelter construction.

Timber carrier

One AMC crew member developed an attachment for a rock bar that allows it to be used like a peavey or cant dog. It can be used for rolling logs or twisting the base of a felled tree that has gotten hung up in another tree and must be knocked loose. The latter procedure, or course, should be done with utmost care.

Rock bar with cant dog

Packboard

The AMC has developed a packboard (see pp. 224–25 for detailed plan) used for resupplying its hut system and packing tools and supplies into the field for a week at a time. Rugged and heavy duty, if not comfortable, it has survived many years of hard service. Its main purpose is to carry heavy loads (80 to 120 pounds) over relatively short distances (3 to 5 miles). It is included here for those maintainers planning heavy-duty reconstruction work.

The frame is made of straight-grained white ash, a strong and resilient wood that can withstand the stresses and strains of heavy loads.

The following is a list of the other materials needed:

a) Oak leather pieces for tote harness—26" long x 2 1/2" wide, 9/64" to 10/64" thick, oil dressed.

b) 1" copper rivets with burrs, 6–10 gauge (sub 7/8").

c) No. 414 nickel buckle with imitation roller, 1 1/4

d) pack corset

Aluminum pack frames can be purchased from camping and hunting suppliers. Essentially this is an external-frame pack without an attached pack. Although not as rugged as the custom-made wooden packboard, these have proven capable of carrying heavy loads and adjusting to fit people of all sizes.

Safety Equipment

Besides the various sheaths used to protect blades and users, a variety of safety equipment is available.

Hard hats come in many styles, colors, and materials. Strong and comfortable hats that meet ANSI Z89.1-1986 standards for impact should be selected. Color, though seemingly insignificant, can make a difference, as white or aluminum-colored ones are much cooler than dark ones on hot summer days.

Steel-toed boots are recommended for chain-saw work. Also available are *chaps* or *leggings* and *chest pads* made of very strong but lightweight mesh, much like a bulletproof vest, that give the chain-saw user some margin of protection from cuts.

Safety goggles or *face masks* are appropriate in chain-saw work and when using a brush cutter or jackhammer. *Hearing protectors* are also available and should be used for ear protection when operating motorized tools.

Shin guards used by baseball catchers are sometimes used by maintainers engaged in extensive ax work and digging with mattocks. *Leather work gloves* are preferred by some to protect hands from blisters and cuts.

Don't Lose Your Tools

Used wood and metal hand tools quickly become drab and easily blend into trailside brush and woods. Remember where you left them and keep them close by or on the trail. At the end of the work day gather up all the crew's tools and make sure they are accounted for. Keep tools in one stash or cache at camp or near the work site, just out of sight of the trail. To help keep tools from "hiding" in the brush, liberally paint a good portion of the heads and handles with a brightly colored paint like orange or red. Do not paint the cutting or digging edges of the heads or the gripping parts of the handles.

Tool Sources

Tools can be purchased at hardware stores and from catalogs and outlets of forestry, farm, and construction equipment suppliers. Look for inexpensive used tools at garage sales, used tool outlets, and antique shops. Often the best wood-cutting hand tools, like axes and crosscut saws, were made decades ago.

Plan for AMC packboard.

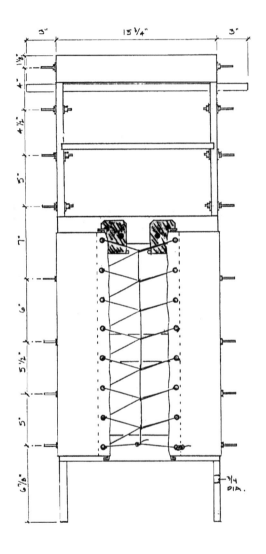

3/16" thick leather from Limmer & Sons — Intervale, N.H.

All wood joinery glued and screwed.

Rivets: 3/8" diameter, available at Covs & Drew, Inc. — North Plymouth, Mass.

Corset: use heavy-duty canvas and brass grommets.

All dadoes 1/4".

Grommets: 1/4" inside diameter available with canvas corsets at Ragged Mountain Works, Intervale, N.H.

Finish: Polyeurethane or stain and poly. Sand well and ease all edges 1/8".

Hooks: 3/16" stock, 7/8" O.D. eye hooks with 5/8" openings cut in one side to form C-hook for pack rope.

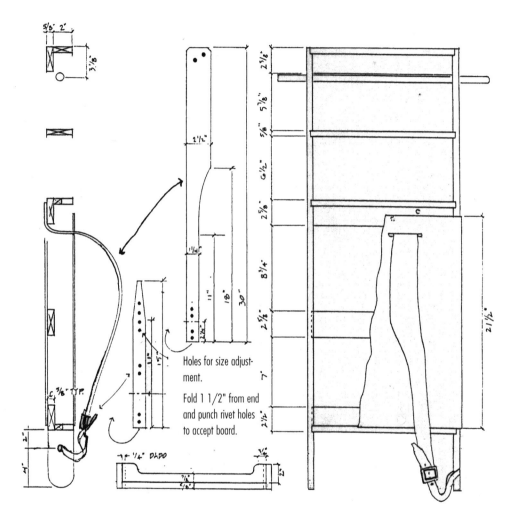

Holes for size adjustment.

Fold 1 1/2" from end and punch rivet holes to accept board.

CHAPTER ELEVEN
Developing and Using Trail Maintenance Inventories

A measuring wheel and a microcassette recorder can be used to produce highly detailed reports of trail conditions and work needs.

Inventories or assessments of trail conditions and maintenance needs are useful in a variety of ways to trail maintainers, land managers, and others. They can be used for short-term and long-range planning; for scheduling maintenance; for budget preparation; for prioritizing projects; and for guiding trail maintainers or assigning them to certain tasks.

Trail Surveys

Use a simple trail condition survey to assess gross maintenance needs and to identify specific trail problems. Most maintainers use one in the spring to prepare for the summer maintenance effort. The AMC trail crew hikes all AMC trails in the White Mountains in the spring to remove winter blowdowns and identify trail problems; the crew leaders then fill out a "patroller's report" (see form A) for each trail. Trail adopters also file reports on minor and major maintenance needs (see form B).

TRAIL CONDITION REPORT
AMC TRAILS PROGRAM

DATE:_____

NAME:_____

TRAIL: SECTION:

CREW (list names):
Leader:

REPORTED DURING:
- ❏ Patrolling   ❏ Signing
- ❏ Inspection   ❏ Other:

Please Comment on <u>All</u> the Following Observations:

WEATHER CONDITIONS (During Inspection):

GENERAL TRAIL CONDITION (Due to Recent Weather):
❏ Very Wet   ❏ Wet   ❏ Normal   ❏ Dry   ❏ Frozen   ❏ Other:

BLAZES:

<u>Condition</u>	<u>Quality</u>	<u>Quantity</u>	<u>Color</u>	Note Problems and Solutions:
❏ Good	❏ Neat	❏ Right	❏ White	
❏ Fair	❏ Messy	❏ Too Few	❏ Yellow	
❏ Bad	❏ Big/Small	❏ Too Many	❏ Blue	

BRUSHING (Standardizing) CONDITION: Note Problem Locations and Lengths:
❏ Good   ❏ Needs Some (Soon)
❏ Too Wide   ❏ Needs a Lot (Now)

GENERAL DRAINAGE MAINTENANCE CONDITION: Note Problems and Locations:
❏ Clean (Good or Done)   ❏ Needs Normal Cleaning
❏ Needs Extensive Cleaning   ❏ Needs Rebuilding

USE (By Hikers):   ❏ Low   ❏ Moderate   ❏ High   ❏ Can't Tell

OVERALL TRAIL SECTION CONDITION AND PRIORITY:

<u>Condition</u>	<u>Priority for Work</u>	
❏ Great	= Low	-Needs little or no work (annual maintenance; clean drainages, brush, blaze, etc.) - Adt.
❏ Good	= Low/Med	-Needs some minor work later, stable for now (replace & add a few WB, RS, SS, etc.) - VC, Adt.
❏ Fair	= Med	-Needs some work soon to control moderate damage (some RS, SS, BB, drainages, etc.) - VC, TC
❏ Bad	= Med/High	-Needs abundant work now to repair and stop damage (lots of rock work, WB, SS, BB) - TC, VC
❏ Very Bad	= High	-Needs major work now to repair and stop much serious damage (major reconstruction/relo) - TC

Problems, Work Needed, and Locations (Please Be Specific)

Drainage Needs: Is there running water, erosion, wet areas, etc., that can be repaired or controlled by replacing, improving, and/or installing additional drainages? What's the problem and location?

_____

_____

What type of drainage is needed (rocks, water bars, wood water bars, dips, ditches, etc.), how many of each are needed, and where?

_____

_____

Trail Tread Stability Needs: Are there trail tread problems or erosion that require replacing, improving, and/or installing additional rock steps, cribbing, sidehilling, etc.? What's the problem and location?

_____

_____

What type of stability work is needed, how many of each are needed, and where?

_____

_____

Trail Hardening Needs: Are there muddy, boggy, or other undrainable areas that require trail hardening such as replacing, improving, and/or installing additional step stones, bog bridges, turnpikes, etc.? What's the problem, length, and location?

_____

_____

What type of hardening is needed, how many of each are needed, and where?

_____

_____

Trail Defining and Marking Needs: Are there sections that are difficult to follow, are too wide, have bootlegs, etc., that require better signs, cairns, blazes, scree walls, brushing in, etc.? What and where are the problems and what type, quantity, and length of work is needed?

_____

_____

Special Needs: Are there any such as streams, difficult stream crossings, ladders, difficult ledges, bootleg campsites, trailhead problems, etc.? Please elaborate on problem(s) and solution(s).

_____

_____

WORK REPORT
AMC TRAILS PROGRAM

Project Date: ___/___/___ thru: ___/___/___

Name:_____

Trail: _____ Section: _____

Program: ☐ Staff Trail Crew ☐ Camp Dodge Crew ☐ Other:_____

Crew

Names	Hours	Names	Hours
Leader:			

NEW WORK COMPLETED

New Work Installed or Existing Work Replaced									
Type	#	Feet	Type	#	Feet	Type	#	Feet	OFD Ft.
Rock Step (RS)			Bog Bridge [Native] (BBN)			Rock Water Bar (RWB)			
Step Stone (SS)			Bog Bridge [Lumber] (BBL)			Wood Water Bar (WWB)			
Cairn (CRN)			Rock Cribbing (RCB)			Dip (DIP)			
Log Step (LS)			Log Cribbing (LCB)			Bleeder (BLD)			
Scree Wall (SCR)			Stream Bridge (SB)			Cross Ditch (CD)			
Brush-in (BI)			Ladder (LDR)			Ditch (DCH)			OFD= Outflow Ditch (i.e., off end of WB)
Sidehill (SH)			Turnpike (TP)			Outsloping (OS)			
						Stream Channeling (SCH)			

Note any other new work installed that is not listed above, such as: cut new relo, hung sign, fixed ledge, etc. Be sure to include number and feet (or miles).

_____

_____

_____

(over)

MAINTENANCE WORK COMPLETED (Please be specific)

Existing Work Improved, Repaired, or Reset							Drainage Control		
Type	#	Feet	Type	#	Feet	OFD Ft	#	Feet	OFD Ft.
Rock Step (RS)			Rock Water Bar (RWB)						
Step Stone (SS)			Wood Water Bar (WWB)						
Cairn (CRN)			Dip (DIP)						
Bog Bridge [Native] (BBN)			Bleeder (BLD)						
Bog Bridge [Lumber] (BBL)			Cross Ditch (CD)						
Scree Wall (SCR)			Ditch (DCH)			OFD = Outflow Ditch (i.e., off end of WB)			OFD = Outflow Ditch (i.e., off end of WB)
Sidehill (SH)			Rock Cribbing (RCB)						
			Log Cribbing (LCB)						

Basic Maintenance							
Type	#	Miles	Type	Miles or Ft.	Type	Miles	Color
Blowdown Removed			Brushing (Standardizing)		Blazing		

Note any other **maintenance work completed** not listed above, such as: removed trip roots, removed old bog bridges, closed bootleg campsite, etc. Be sure to include number and feet (or miles).

_____

_____

_____

_____

_____

Thanks!

Most trail groups have their own assessment forms to collect information on specific problems (e.g., a missing sign) or general maintenance needs (e.g., a boggy or eroded section of trail). Specific problems may require a follow-up field check to thoroughly assess the situation and prepare for eventual correction. Some forms provide for comments about guidebook descriptions; assessment of facilities along the trail; parking accommodations; observations on off-trail or bootleg camping; and other trail-related matters. Some also double as work reports.

Bear in mind that the degree of detail provided will vary depending on the specific questions asked and the trail maintenance experience of the person doing the inventory. Those not trained in trail problems and their solutions can find help in various trails manuals such as this book, the *Appalachian Trail Field Book: A Self-Help Guide for Trail Maintainers* (developed by the Appalachian Trail Conference), or the Student Conservation Association's *Lightly on the Land*.

Assessment quality depends on the training and observation of the person doing the survey. Someone familiar with a trail may not mention sparse blazes, whereas someone on a trail for the first time may have a hard time following it and feel it is underblazed. Someone else may view a particular gully or other trail problem as standard and not mention it, while another might note it as a problem. Get input from both maintainers and hikers to make up for the biases if only one or two evaluations are considered.

Creating Work Logs

Detailed inventories of trail maintenance and construction needs generated by one or more people experienced in all aspects of trail work are very helpful for quantifying work or preparing for large projects. Such inventories, or work logs, point out very specific solutions for each trail problem encountered and utilize a reference point system as a guide for trail crews. Work logs are especially helpful for prioritizing and scheduling projects, and estimating time and expenses required.

Work logs should be prepared by experienced trail people. Two people are ideal because their expertise and knowledge can be combined to evaluate and develop a prescription for a difficult trail problem. Generate work logs while traveling uphill; the view of treadway is better when going uphill at a slow pace than when walking downhill, when people travel at a faster pace and are preoccupied with footing. Spring is the best time to do work logs and see water-related problems that might not be evident in summer or fall.

Good detailed work logs take time. On a trail requiring extensive work, it may take an experienced person a full day to log three or four miles.

For equipment, all you need is a notebook and pencil, a micro-cassette recorder, and a measuring wheel. Engineer's field books with waterproof paper provide the best writing medium. Use a mechanical pencil to avoid smeared ink. With waterproof paper and a mechanical pencil, you'll be able to take clear, legible notes even in the heaviest downpour. Use the notebook to record relevant details or sketches to supplement the work log.

Test the recorder to be sure it is working properly, and check it frequently. Don't reach the end of the trail to find only a quarter of the report on tape. Bring extra batteries and tapes and a zip-lock bag for the recorder in case it rains—you can record and control the recorder through the plastic. Write out your notes if the recorder fails. A clinometer or abney level is handy for estimating slopes.

Wherever you plan to start, record the name of the trail; date; names of those generating the log; weather conditions and when it last rained; the wheel conversion rate if any; and a description of the exact location of where the log begins.

Then head uphill, holding the microcassette recorder in one hand

and the measuring wheel in the other. When you get to a distinctive feature or problem, take a moment to thoroughly analyze the problem and propose a solution. Think about how you will describe it verbally before recording. Then turn the recorder on, note your location by reading the number on the wheel, and, speaking clearly and crisply, briefly describe the problem and a specific, quantified solution. For example, "Install an eight-foot rock water bar draining right." List all trail junctions, streams, and outlooks. Where work is widely scattered, give a reference like: "Install fifteen-foot wood waterbar draining left, ten feet below large white birch with blaze on right; two big boulders on left just above water bar location." The more detail, the better. At the end of the trail or section you log, record a brief summary of the trail condition and the work needed. Transcribe the work log directly off the tape.

Developing a work log with a measuring wheel with five-foot increments provides crews with distances that can be easily estimated, paced, and computed without a wheel. If you record your measurements carefully and are certain to note the location of easily distinguished features, the person or crew using the log will be able to locate specifically referenced maintenance needs with great accuracy.

Using a Work Log

If a trail crew is to do work as outlined specifically in a work log, waterproof the log for field use with contact paper or a large ziplock bag. Someone on the crew should ideally help develop the log, so there will be direct input from those who have done and will be doing the work. This will help the crew understand the work instructions and the rationale behind them. Should someone from the crew not be able to assist the person who does develop the work log, the latter should provide clear work descriptions and cite detailed references. Since no work log can ever be considered completely accurate or absolutely the best prescription for every trail problem—two logs done by the same person for the same trail at different times will vary—flexible procedures should be planned to accommodate the variations from the work log.

To save time for the work crew, flag the work on the trail shortly before the project begins. Use flagging tape to mark each location where work is needed, and write on each piece of tape either the instruction (e.g., three rock steps) or a reference point from the log using a permanent marking pen. If flagging or wooden stakes are used, do not place them in the field too long in advance of when the work will be done. Hikers may remove some, because they are too distracting. Others may simply vandalize them. Remove all flagging and stakes when the work is completed.

Detailed work logs are invaluable in prioritizing work projects and estimating time and expense involved. Setting priorities can be done by both type and quantity of problems, considering such factors as use levels and when the trail was last worked on. A low-use trail with a small but severe erosion problem may be of lower priority than a heavily used trail with a long boggy section. Logs with brief narratives about the nature of the trail sections (e.g., "gully 3 feet wide and 1 foot deep versus 1 foot deep") can also be of help in decision making. A steep section of trail with extensive gullies needing 100 water bars is probably a higher priority than a trail following an old logging road on a gentle grade that needs 100 water bars over its entire length.

To estimate time and expense involved, you must know through regular record-keeping what amount of work is produced on the average (e.g., fifty bog bridges per four-person crew per week). You can then extrapolate to another trail section. For example, 200 bridges would likely require four weeks for the crew described above. The cost of the crew per week can be utilized to compute an average cost per work item, which can in turn be used to estimate the cost of completing a large project. A simple tally sheet on which numbers of work items can be placed will facilitate estimates.

As trails change over time, detailed work logs might be quickly outdated. The AMC crews have found little change overall in tread condition on most trails over a few years, but conditions always get worse, never better. Trail conditions can change considerably if use levels change dramatically or a natural catastrophe occurs (e.g., a landslide, or a stream jumps its course and floods the trail). The work prescription should be similar over time, with slightly more work needed. For planning purposes, work logs should prove to be good for quite a few years. However, work logs should not be done too far in advance of when the work will begin.

Trail work histories are very helpful for the maintainer. Knowing when work was done enables the maintainer to gauge the life span of various construction and maintenance techniques. Some techniques may be longer lasting than others; knowing how long work lasts helps with long-range planning and budgeting for future reconstruction.

APPENDIX A

Personal First-Aid Kit for the Trail Worker

- 1 package of moleskin or molefoam
- aspirin or ibuprofen
- 1 triangular bandage and safety pins
- an assortment of band-aids
- 1 Ace bandage
- 3 4" x 4" gauze dressings
- 1 roll of tape or Kling bandage
- gloves
- pocket mask
- antihistamine capsules
- iodine antiseptic or iodine antiseptic wipes
- shears or scissors

APPENDIX B

First-Aid Kit for a Trail Crew of up to Ten Persons

- 1 roll of tape
- 4 triangular bandages and safety pins
- 3 3" Kling bandages
- 6 4" x 4" gauze pads
- 15 band-aids
- 2 packages of moleskin or molefoam
- 1 pair of bandage scissors
- 1 pair of tweezers
- 2 5" x 9" combine dressings
- 1 sam splint
- 2 Ace bandages

- 1 pen
- 5 "soap" notes or incident report forms
- 1 pocket mask
- 1 eye wash
- 1 bottle of iodine antiseptic
- 12 ibuprofen
- 6 pairs of gloves
- 1 tube of glucose
- 1 cold pack

and

- a leader trained in backcountry first aid

APPENDIX C

Suppliers of Tools, Equipment, and Materials for Trail Work

This list is not complete; the companies listed are some of the ones that AMC purchases tools and other supplies from most frequently. Many of the more common tools can be purchased from hardware stores, home supply centers, or other specialty stores closer to you. Companies in **bold** are wholesalers and/or manufacturers and may sell direct, but only in multiple quantities. These brands can be found or ordered at many hardware stores, or you can call the company for the name of a local dealer.

American Coding & Marking Ink, *1220 North Ave., Plainfield, NJ 07062.* ACMI manufactures a brushable ink that we have found to be excellent for blazes.

Ben Meadows Company, *P.O. Box 80549, Atlanta, GA 30366; 800-241-6401 (orders and tech support), 800-628-2068 (fax); www.benmeadows.com.* Ben Meadows, like Forestry Suppliers, sells many of the tools and supplies a trail worker might need. For a catalog, call their 800 number.

Forestry Suppliers, Inc., *205 West Rankin St., P.O. Box 8397, Jackson, MS 39284-8397; 800-647-5368 (orders), 800-543-4203 (fax); www.forestry-suppliers.com.* Forestry Suppliers, like Ben Meadows, sells many of the tools and supplies a trail worker might need. For a catalog, call 800-360-7788.

Griphoist Division of Tractel, Inc., *392 University Ave., P.O. Box 68, Westwood, MA 02090; 800-421-0246, 781-329-6530 (fax).* AMC uses the griphoist most often with rock work, but recognizes it as an extremely durable and useful tool all around. Call for a brochure to locate the dealer closest to you.

Labonville, Inc., 504 Main St., Gorham, NH 03581; 603-752-4030, 603-752-7621 (fax); www.labonville.com. Labonville is an honest-to-goodness North Woods logging supply company, with a long history of selling top-quality safety gear and clothing for the logger, as well as a full line of work and outdoor clothing, boots, tools, and other gear. Call for a copy of their mail-order catalog.

Leetonia Tool Co., 142 Main St., Leetonia, OH 44431; 330-427-6944, 330-427-6128 (fax). Leetonia makes many "high-grade construction, hardware, and marine tools." For the trail worker, Leetonia makes pick mattocks, picks, cutter mattocks, rock bars (which they call wedge point or pinch point crow bars), tampers, and other specialty tools. Their tools are very rugged and will hold up to many years of hard use. You'll need to buy in the quantity they ship, usually a half-dozen. All Leetonia tools are made in the USA.

Sequatchie Handle Works, Inc., Sequatchie, TN 37374; 800-221-3419, 423-942-6806 (fax). Sequatchie makes handles for striking and edge tools, farming, industrial tools, shovels, scoops, spades, mallets, and handles for other tools. Sequatchie's handle selection is truly impressive and their workmanship is excellent. Will sell and ship handles by the dozen only.

Snow & Nealley Co., P.O. Box 876, Bangor, ME 04402-0876; 207-947-6642, 207-941-0857 (fax). Snow & Nealley makes what we believe to be the best single-bit ax on the market today. In fact, new trails department employees are issued new Snow & Nealley 3 1/2-pound axes as part of their orientation. S&N also makes draw shaves, bark spuds, broad axes, mauls, cant dogs and hooks, timber tongs, pulp hooks, and pickeroons. Their tools are American made and carry a lifetime warranty.

Voss Signs, P.O. Box 553, Manlius, NY 13104; 315-682-6418, 315-682-7335 (fax). Voss manufactures stock and custom aluminum and plastic signs and markers for forests, parks, wildlife preserves, private property, and other applications. They specialize in custom signs and have complete typesetting and art facilities.

GLOSSARY

backfill Mineral soil used to support a drainage structure. Backfill is used behind (downtrail) a rock or log water bar, or to reinforce a drainage dip.

basic maintenance (annual maintenance) Involves four tasks, listed in order of priority: cleaning drainage, clearing blowdowns, brushing, and blazing or marking. All should be done annually or more as needed.

berm A mound of soil that runs parallel to a trail on the downslope side. Often found on old roads or on eroded trails. Berms generally must be penetrated to allow for proper drainage.

bog bridge (puncheon, topped log bridge) A simple bridge constructed of two base logs (or sills) set perpendicular to the trail and two stringers, parallel to the trail and spiked to the top of the base logs.

buffer zone The land area on each side of the trail treadway. Buffer zones shield the hiker from activities such as second-home development, mining, or logging that are detrimental to the hiking experience.

Circle of Danger The area surrounding the worker that is unsafe due to tool use. The inner (or primary) circle of danger is the area the tool can reach while the worker is using it. The outer circle of danger is the area the tool could reach if the worker lost control or let go of the tool.

crump To break, crush, or cause to fail tools, equipment, or fingers. Also, to set down a heavy pack load prior to collapsing from exhaustion.

definers Used to channel or focus foot traffic onto a hardened or harder tread, thus protecting soils that may be wet, thin, or supporting fragile plant life. Scree and rock steps are examples of definers.

drainage Devices or structures, such as water bars, drainage dips, and ditches, that remove water from the trail tread or prevent water from entering the tread and thus limit or eliminate the effects of erosion.

duffing The preparation of the trail tread for foot traffic. Involves scraping away any organic materials (the O1 layer, or duff)—leaves, needles, roots, bark, and decomposing vegetation—and any organic soil (O2 or decomposed organic materials).

easement Grants a nonowner the right to use a specific portion of land for a specific purpose. Easements may be limited to a specific period of time or may be granted in perpetuity; or, the termination of the easement may be predicated upon the occurrence of a specific event. An easement agreement survives transfer of landownership and is generally binding upon future owners until it expires on its own terms.

erosion control Includes work or devices designed to control surface erosion (drainages, hardeners, definers, and stabilizers).

five fundamentals of preparation The right protective gear, the right food and water, the right plan and tools, the right training, and the right attitude. Even a short work trip requires the five fundamentals of preparation.

grade A measurement of the rate of rise of a trail, road, or slope. Expressed as a percentage. A trail that rises 9 vertical feet in 100 horizontal feet has a 9 percent grade. Grade is different from angle; angle is measured with a straight vertical as 90 degrees and straight horizontal as 0 degrees. A grade of 100 percent would have an angle of 45 degrees.

hardeners Objects used to eliminate the impact of foot travel through wet areas. Hardeners include bog bridges, step stones, and turnpiking (constructing a raised tread).

lease The grant of an interest in land upon payment of a determined fee. The fee does not have to be monetary, but some consideration must be given for the right to use the land or the lease will not be legally binding.

license Allows the licensed party to enter the land of the licensor without being deemed a trespasser.

mineral soil Found below the organic horizon, mineral soil is comprised of clays, silts, sands, and other inorganic materials. Mineral soils generally provide a stable and durable treadway when properly drained.

oral agreement Generally, a contract involving the sale of real estate is not binding unless it is in writing. Therefore an oral agreement that actually transfers ownership of land is not legally binding. Although some types of agreements for the use of land need not be written, an oral agreement will always be difficult to enforce because the parties may disagree over the original terms of their contract. An oral agreement is therefore inappropriate for use in a trail project except during the preliminary planning stages.

organic soil From the organic soil horizons, organic soil is made up of leaves, needles, plants, roots, bark, and other organic material in various stages of decay, and has a large water/mass absorption ratio.

outflow The off-treadway ditch portion of a drainage structure, intended to remove all water from the trail.

outslope The grade from the upslope edge of the treadway to the downslope edge. Trails, especially sidehill trails, should have an outslope of 3 percent to allow for proper sheet drainage.

ownership-in-fee (also known as fee purchase or fee simple) A complete transfer of land ownership from one landowner to another party, usually by purchase.

pin rock A medium-sized rock, usually 150–250 pounds, whose mass is used to anchor a log step or water bar.

pooched Stymied or thwarted.

protective zone See *buffer*.

rubble Rocks smaller than scree, usually 15–75 pounds, used in alpine areas (to slow water in outflow ditches) and other applications.

scree Material used to define a trail and/or channel hiker traffic. Made of medium to large rocks (but also fallen trees or large limbs), scree is set along rock staircases to stabilize soils and direct hiker traffic onto the staircase. Scree is also built into walls in alpine areas to define the treadway and keep hikers off fragile vegetation.

sheet drainage The natural, gravitational progression of rainfall, snowmelt, and widely dispersed surface water down a slope.

sidehill trail or **sidehill construction** A sidehill trail, often literally cut out of the side of a hill, gains elevation by moving up a slope, gradually following the contour. To avoid a gully or ravine, a sidehill trail will turn in the opposite direction by using a switchback. Sidehill trails are well suited for accessible trails, trails used by pack animals, or other applications where a trail's grade must be limited.

stabilizers Used to hold soil in place and prevent erosion from water, feet, gravity, or other forces. Stabilizers include rock steps (used to stabilize steep gullied or eroding slopes) and cribbing (used to anchor soil above or below a trail on a slope).

switchback Used to gain elevation on sidehill trails. The switchback is a sharp turn in the opposite direction.

terminuses The trailhead or start of the trail (usually at roadside) and the destination (a mountain summit, waterfall, mill site, or similar feature).

trail *Webster's New World Dictionary* defines a trail as "a blazed or trodden path through a wild region," but it's more than that; a good trail also protects the region it passes through from damage.

trail corridor Includes the treadway, right of way, buffer zones, and all the lands that make up the environment of the trail as experienced by the hiker. The Forest Service has called it the "zone of travel influence."

trail landscape See *trail corridor*.

trail right of way The area around the treadway that is cleared for the passage of the hiker. It is usually four to six feet wide, depending on vegetation density. If a trail has other uses besides hiking, such as cross-country skiing or mountain biking, the right of way will likely be wider. The term "right of way" also refers to legal right of passage, as would be the case with a protected trail on private land.

trail treadway or **trail tread** The surface on which the hiker makes direct contact with the ground. It is the location for virtually all improvements intended to conserve soil resources.

RECOMMENDED READING

Birchard, William, Jr., and Robert D. Proudman. *Trail Design, Construction, and Maintenance*, 2d ed. Harpers Ferry, WV: Appalachian Trail Conference, 1998. 210 pp. Available at 304-535-6331.

Birkby, Robert C. *Lightly on the Land: The Student Conservation Association Trail-Building and Maintenance Manual.* Seattle, WA: The Mountaineers. ISBN 0-89886-491-7. 272 pp. Available at 800-553-4453.

Doucette, Joseph E., and Kenneth D. Kimball. *Passive Trail Management in Northeastern Alpine Zones: A Case Study.* In: More, T. A., et al., eds. "Proceedings of the 1990 Northeastern Recreation Research Symposium," Saratoga Springs, NY, Feb. 25–28, 1990. U.S. Forest Service, General Tech. Report NE-145:195–201.

Griswold, Stephen. *Trail Handbook: Sequoia and Kings Canyon National Parks.* Three Rivers, CA: U.S. Department of Interior, National Park Service, 1991. 86 pp. Available at 209-565-3795.

Hallman, Richard. "Handtools for Trailwork." Gen. Tech. Rep. 8823-2601-MTDC. Missoula, MT: U.S. Department of Agriculture, Forest Service, Missoula Technology and Development Center, 1988. 26 pp. Available at 406-329-3900.

Hesselbarth, Woody, and Brian Vachowski. "Trail Construction and Maintenance Notebook." Tech. Rep. 9623-2833-MTDC. Missoula, MT: U.S. Department of Agriculture, Forest Service, Missoula Technology and Development Center, 1996. 139 pp.

Miller, Warren. "Crosscut Saw Manual." Gen. Tech. Rep. 7771-2508-MTDC. Missoula, MT: U.S. Department of Agriculture, Forest Service, Missoula Technology and Development Center, 1988. 28 pp. Available at 406-329-3900.

INDEX

Pants, 5
Paper cup, 80
Parking/trailhead facilities, planning, 42–43
Pick, use and care of, 213
Pick mattock
    drainage cleaning and, 66
    erosion control and, 132, 148
    rock moving and, 98
    use and care of, 211
Planning process, new-trail
    overview of, 41–42
    roads and private land, 43–44
    for ski-touring (cross-country) trails,
        174–75
    soils, 47–57
    switchbacks, 44–47
    topography, 44
    trailhead/parking facilities, 42–43
Pole clippers, use and care of, 204–5
Pole saw, 71
Posts, instead of cairns, 93, 95
Power tools, use and care of, 215–20.
    See also individual tools
Private land
    concerns of landowners, 29–37
    determining, 21–23
    legal arrangements to establish
        trail right of way, 26–29
    new-trail layout and, 43–44
    overview of, 20
    talking to landowners, 25–26
    types and patterns of, 23–25
Pruners, hand, 71
    use and care of, 204–6
Pruning saw, use and care of, 202–3
Pulaski ax, 199

Rag, 80
Rain gear, 5
Rake, fire, 66
    use and care of, 213
Reconstruction of trails, building
    materials/techniques for
        overview of, 96
        rock, moving, 98–102, 104–10
        rock, selecting, 97–98
        service trails, 96
        soil for fill, 97
        trees, using, 110–16
Reconstruction of trails, erosion control and.
    See Erosion control, trail-reconstruction
Relocation vs. repair of trail, 117–19, 144–45
Roads, new-trail layout and, 43
Rock, moving
    barricades and, 100
    cutting, 110
    with hand tools, 98–100
    safety considerations, 99–100, 109
    tools for, 98–102, 104–10
    winches/hoisting equipment and,
        100–102, 108–9
Rock, selecting, 97–98
Rock bar, 98, 132, 148
    use and care of, 213

Rock drill, use and care of, 220
Rock treadways, 146
Root ax, 66, 132, 148
Router/routing, signs and, 86, 88–89

Safety ax, use and care of, 208–9
Safety considerations
    chain-saw, 3–5, 217–19
    first-aid kits, 6, 236
    rock-moving, 99–100, 109
    skyline-technique, 109
    tree-felling, 113–14
Saw. *See Bow saw; Chain saw; Crosscut saw;
    Pole saw*
Scree walls, 154–57
Scrench, 112
Scrub pad, 79, 80
Service trails, 96
Shovel
    drainage cleaning and, 66
    erosion control and, 132, 148
    use and care of, 210
Signs
    hanging, 90–92
    making wooden routed, 86–90
    master list for, 92
    other types of, 92–93
    overview of, 85–86
    for ski-touring (cross-country) trails,
        187–88
    temporary, 92
    tools for, 88–90
Single-line pull, 104–5
Single-span stringer bridges, 160–64
Ski-touring (cross-country) trails
    bridges and stream crossings, 183–87
    construction process, 179–83
    facilities for, 188
    gradient of, 182–83
    height of, 180
    layout of, 175–76, 178
    length of, 183
    location considerations, 178–79
    mapping for, 187–88
    marking systems for, 187–88
    overview of, 172–74
    planning and design of, 174–75
    tracks, 173
    tread for, 180–82
    width of, 179–80
Skyline technique
    safety considerations, 109
    setup, 106–8
    tools for, 105
Sledgehammer, 112, 141, 148
Socks, 2–3
Soil, for trail-reconstruction fill, 97
Soils, new-trail layout and
    compaction, 48
    depth, 52–53
    erosion, 48–49
    horizons, 54–57
    overview of, 47
    texture, 51–52

00054

6 52932 01495 4